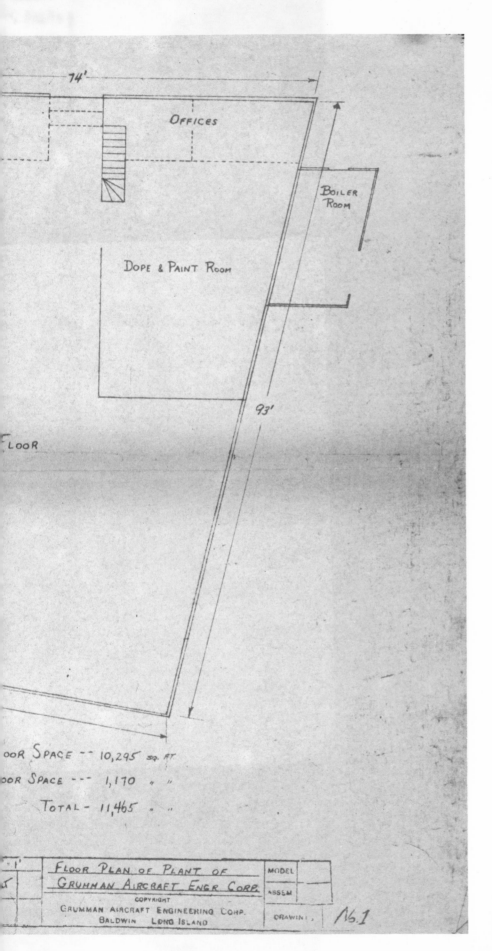

74'

OFFICES

BOILER
ROOM

DOPE & PAINT ROOM

93'

FLOOR

OOR SPACE -- 10,295 SQ. FT.

OOR SPACE --- 1,170 " "

TOTAL - 11,465 " "

FLOOR PLAN OF PLANT OF	MODEL	
GRUMMAN AIRCRAFT ENGR CORP.	ASSEM	
COPYRIGHT GRUMMAN AIRCRAFT ENGINEERING CORP. BALDWIN LONG ISLAND	DRAWING	No. 1

From these humble beginnings in Baldwin, N.Y. Grumman has now grown into one of the world's leading aerospace corporations.

One of a Kind

To the memory of Chuck Sewell – Grumman Corporation's chief test pilot from 1971 to 1986 – and to all the aviators, beginning with Leroy Grumman, whose skill, courage and dedication have helped to create the world's foremost family of aircraft.

One of a Kind

The story of Grumman

Bill Gunston

This book was devised and produced by TRH Pictures and Chevprime Ltd.

Design and Production: Derek Avery
Picture Research: TRH Pictures

The editorial content of "One of a Kind" was determined solely by the author, who was assisted by Grumman Corporation with research relating to Grumman products and company history.

ISBN 0 517 56796 2

Printed in Hong Kong by Toppan Printing Co Ltd

First published in 1988 by
TRH Pictures and Chevprime Ltd
London, England.

Contents

Prosperity in the Depression

The Grumman story has its roots in the formation of another company entirely. In 1917 America's desperate need was for airplanes, and one of the nation's few qualified aeronautical engineers, Grover C. Loening, started his own planemaking business in a loft in New York City. He handled the engineering design himself, but in October 1920 he persuaded Lt. Leroy Randle Grumman to leave the Navy and join him as plant manager and test pilot. Four years later he hired two more men whose ability had impressed him: Leon A. "Jake" Swirbul came as production supervisor and William T. "Bill" Schwendler, as an engineering problem-solver.

In 1928 Loening sold out, and a year later the new owners planned to move operations to Bristol, Pennsylvania. Grumman, Swirbul and Schwendler looked for some way of staying in New York and gradually began to consider forming their own company – to build airplanes, of course. Wealthy Loening was prepared to help, and once Grumman had signed up the Loening bookkeeper and assistant treasurer, Ed Poor (a most cautious man with finance), he felt he had enough to get started. Through 1929 Grumman and his friends began handpicking men from the Loening workforce. In the late fall of that year the stock market crashed and the Depression set in.

One man who found himself looking for work was Clint Towl, a friend of Poor's. He wasn't bothered at the prospect of a small salary: he was prepared to invest in the proposed Grumman Aircraft Engineering Corporation provided he could have a job. So, on December 5, 1929, Loening and his brother Albert, Grumman, Swirbul, Poor and Towl signed the stock agreement totalling $77,250, of which $58,825 was actually available (a short time later, Schwendler also invested). The new company was incorporated on the following day.

The company's new plant was a derelict garage in Baldwin, on Long

Previous pages: From these humble beginnings in Baldwin, N.Y. Grumman has now grown into one of the world's leading aerospace corporations.

Below: Interior of the Baldwin plant at the start of manufacturing operations; on the left, a float; on the right, Loening wings.

Left: Founders of the firm at Bethpage in 1940: from the left, Leroy Grumman, Bill Schwendler and Leon "Jake" Swirbul.

Island's southern shore about 20 miles from Manhattan. It was in a terrible state, and knee-deep in oak leaves, but on January 2, 1930, the Grumman firm opened for business. But what business? In the closing months of their work for Loening, Grumman and Schwendler had been sketching ideas for a seaplane float incorporating retractable wheels. Loening had built amphibians, but the wheels had merely been raised out of the water, the gear continuing to be dragged through the air. What was wanted – most urgently for the Navy's Vought Corsair scout – was a neat gear that would fold completely into the float. Soon an acceptable amphibian gear existed, but only on paper.

To earn a little money, Grumman decided to seek contracts to repair various crashed or unairworthy Loenings, and before the first week – bitterly cold, in more ways than one – was out, the first wreck had been bought from an insurance company for $400. It was towed to Baldwin behind Grumman's Hudson and parked inside the company's new headquarters. Unfortunately, though, the airplane's nose stuck out into the dirt road, and in the winter darkness a motorist crashed into it. A lawsuit was just what the infant firm did not need, and in a world of crashed companies and hungry lawyers they were only too glad to restore the crumpled car to showroom condition. Then they did the same to the Loening, selling it for $20,000. But what they really wanted was to land a Navy contract for their amphibious float. For its day, the float was a good example of advanced technology. By employing the new all-metal stressed-skin form of construction, the complete float with landing gear came out on paper lighter than the original Corsair float with no wheels. The float incorporated a carrier arrester hook, and the wheel gears could be cranked up by hand, or pulled by a hydraulic jack. The gears were then swung up on parallel links until, at the top of their travel, the wheels moved inwards until they were completely recessed.

Opposite upper: Grumman's very first production line, in the Baldwin plant, comprised of Model A floats for the Navy. Amidships can be seen the bays for the retracted wheels.

Above: The later J2F Duck float was a superior job, hydrodynamically, aerodynamically and structurally.

Below: The Grumman company badge issued to Leroy Randle Grumman.

The Navy thought, "Fantastic! But will it work, and will it be tough enough to survive a catapult launch?" Grumman got a $33,700 contract for two floats, and for the first time the magic of Grumman came to life. Nobody knew the company would soon have a reputation for building aircraft so strong that it would be known as "The Grumman Iron Works," and a further reputation for advanced engineering translated from paper to metal at record speed. In the first two weeks of February 1930 there was simply no margin for sluggish performance, or for error. At the end of the second week, Grumman and Swirbul took the floats down to Anacostia for the Navy's test program. Static testing showed only small problems; then one float was attached to a Corsair for a live "cat shot." Both Grumman and Swirbul insisted on being the one to ride in the cockpit, so each took a turn. The result was official adoption of Navy Float Type A.

And there was far more than that. The Navy's primary fighter was the Boeing F4B, whose draggy landing gear helped keep its top speed at 176 mph (283 km/h). Could Grumman, asked the Navy, put its retractable wheels on the F4B? Grumman replied that there was insufficient room for the stowed gear, but that his company was working on the design of an HPTSF (High-Performance Two-Seater Fighter). The Navy showed interest, which hardened through such stages as a wooden model for a wind-tunnel and a full-scale mock-up. But the men on the shop floor had to be paid, and Grumman found a new line of business in making corrosion-free aluminum truck bodies, which were lighter than wood and steel bodies. When anyone, including Grumman and Swirbul, had a spare moment, they helped make truck bodies. Today Grumman makes over 10,000 truck bodies of various sizes every year.

Throughout the little Baldwin plant the chief project was referred to simply as The Plane. It would have been a challenge to any aircraft manufacturer in the world; what it meant to Grumman is obvious. The floats and truck bodies meant that there was money coming in, but never very much. One day while checking the temperature of the bucket of dry ice (solid carbon dioxide) used to freeze the soft aluminum rivets, a riveter dropped the $15 thermometer and broke it. Such a loss cast gloom over the entire company.

No aircraft builder ever kicked off with a tougher project. For a start, the finished article had to meet pages of closely typed Navy requirements. These included the ability to be shot off catapults and slammed back into a carrier's arrester wires, to be thrust along by the most powerful new engine available (the Wright Cyclone nine-cylinder air-cooled radial, initially of 620 and later 750 horsepower) fitted inside one of the new ring cowls developed by the National Advisory Committee for Aeronautics and swinging one of the new high-efficiency aluminum propellers. The airplane also had to carry a heavy load of special mission equipment including a new type of mounting for the defensive gun which was aimed by the backseat observer, and do many other things such as float indefinitely after a sea ditching. Not least of the challenges was that the fuselage and tail were of the innovative stressed skin construction. Moreover, a lawyer would have said the dice were heavily loaded against Grumman in trying to get any kind of fair contract out of

Grumman's firstborn, the prototype XFF-1, outside what seemed
at the time to be a gigantic factory
at Valley Stream.

the Navy, which would make sure every clause in an agreement was in
its own favor. What did Grumman have on its own side? A heavy
measure of individual ability, confidence, experience and team spirit.

Negotiations on The Plane seemed endless, but on March 6, 1931, the
Navy eventually asked for a quotation. For a total price of $73,975,
Grumman agreed to supply the Navy with one XFF-1, the designation
meaning Experimental Fighter Grumman, first model (the code letter
G had been assigned to another company, Great Lakes, but Grumman's
letter, F, was soon to become the most famous in the entire Navy
inventory).

The year 1931 was not only a make-or-break year for The Plane and
for Grumman: it also saw the company firmly establish its own way of
doing things. Perhaps because it started small, and the intimate
personal relationships were sustained between everyone on the payroll,
there was simply no room for obstructive procedures, or any kind of
division of the firm into "us" and "them" groups. The engineers who
did the drawings knew how the parts would be made, and designed
them to be easy to make. The foremen and shop workers began with the
simplest and most direct methods of doing everything. These methods
were to continue even through the company's steady growth in the
1930s and its explosive growth in the 1940s, so that Grumman's
customers, and its rivals, would come visiting to see how the company
managed to achieve so much. The reputation endures to this day.

Above: A rebuilt Canadian Car and Foundry version of the FF-1 shows the insignia of VF-5B, "The Red Rippers." The engine is an R1340 Cyclone.

With a designation like XFF-1, the Grumman firstborn had to become "Fifi." Remarkably small for a powerful two-seater, its smooth metal-skinned body had an enlarged forward fuselage to accommodate the retracted landing gears. This, a major characteristic of early Grumman fighters, later resulted in another name: Fertile Myrtle. But a 200-day delivery schedule left little time for levity, especially as the Navy made no provision for any money up front. Today Grumman is concerned because progress payments, traditionally 90 percent, have been cut to 80 percent. In 1931 not a cent came in on the first airplane contract until it was accepted by the Navy.

Indeed, the Navy's decision in June 1931 to go ahead on a proposed scout version of Fifi, the XSF-1, was not entirely a blessing. Though obviously very welcome, it meant the immediate purchase of twice as much raw material, twice as many subcontracted parts, the hiring of extra men, and, not least, an urgent search for bigger and better premises. In the Depression there were skilled men and good plants in abundance, but Grumman was desperately hard-pressed to find the money from its trickle of floats and truck bodies. The company had no choice: a lot of money had to be spent, and on November 4, 1931, the company moved about eight miles west to an unused Naval Reserve hangar at Curtiss Field, Valley Stream.

By this time The Plane was almost complete. On December 29, a crisp winter day, test pilot Bill McAvoy, a contract pilot from the NACA, gunned the big Cyclone and took the XFF-1 into the blue sky. Soon he was back; the oil filler cap was loose and the windshield was splattered. Then he was off again, and from that moment on the XFF-1 never needed very much tinkering. Brutally tested by the Navy, it performed all the demanded aerobatics and dive pull-outs. And

amazingly, for a two-seater, it clocked 195 mph (314 km/h), compared with the 184 mph (296 km/h) of the F4B-4, the latest and fastest single-seater. Meanwhile, work went ahead on the XSF-1 scout, with one of the two forward-firing machine guns replaced by 45 gallons (170 lit) of extra fuel and a slightly more powerful Cyclone engine. Flown on August 20, 1932, this aircraft reached 207 mph (333 km/h).

By 1932 Grumman seemed to be on the verge of major production orders, which would demand a second expansion into new premises. No such orders had been placed, but there was again no choice but to take the gamble. In November 1932 Grumman moved into a relatively vast plant at Farmingdale, on Conklin Street. The move changed the character of the company. Previously it had been like a family in a crowded room; now it looked like everyone's popular idea of an aircraft company. But at the start the cavernous plant had little inside, and some time before the move, everyone took a two-week layoff because the company's financial reserves were close to zero.

Designation: FF-1
Type: Two-seat carrier-based fighter.
Powerplant: Wright R-1820 Cyclone, 9-cylinder air cooled radial, 700 hp.
Wingspan: 34 ft 6 in.
Length: 24 ft 6 in.
Height: 11 ft 1 in.
Weight: 4,830 lb.
Maximum Speed: 207 mph at 4000 ft.
Ceiling: 21,000 ft.
Range: 920 miles.
Armament: 3 x 0.3-in machine guns.
Crew: 2.
Users: USN.

Left: Bureau No. 9460 was the Navy's first SF-1 scout, outwardly almost identical to the FF-1 two-seat fighter.

Designation; JF-1 DUCK.
Type: Utility amphibian.
Powerplant: Pratt & Whitney R-1830 Twin Wasp, 700 hp; later models Wright R-1820 Cyclone, 900 hp.
Wingspan: 39 ft 0 in.
Length: 34 ft 0 in.
Height: 13ft 11 in. **Weight:** 4,400 lb; later 6,711 lb.
Maximum Speed: 188 mph.
Ceiling: 25,000 ft.
Range: 750 miles.
Armament: Normally none.
Crew: 2/3.
Users: USCG, USMC, USN.

Back in 1931 a new hire, Charlie Tilgner, began detailed stress analysis tests on the amphibious float. The result was a redesign which made the assembly, equipped with smaller wheels, lighter and more streamlined. The Navy immediately took this on board as the Type B float, and in winter 1931-32 this float was used by Grumman as the basis for a new airplane, a utility amphibian to replace the old Loenings. The Navy liked this, too, ordering a prototype with the designation XJF-1. Bigger than the FF-1, it was as robust as its predecessor, though the prototype had a new, slim Pratt & Whitney engine, the 700-hp P & W 1830 Twin Wasp Junior. Able to do almost anything, the JF-1 later went into production with the husky 1830 engine. Some went to the Marines, and others to civil customers for such duties as jungle exploration and missionary and medical transport. Despite its utilitarian duties, a later model—the J2F, equipped with a Wright 1820 Cyclone engine—set an amphibian speed record at 191 mph (307 km/h), and with the service name Duck successive models stayed in production until near the end of World War II.

Right: The penultimate J2F-2 to be delivered, with Navy markings showing it to be the 24th (and probably last) airplane in the second Utility squadron (VJ-2). The photograph was probably taken in 1939.

Below: Final assembly of a Cyclone-engined J2F Duck.

At last, just before Christmas 1932, the Navy placed a production order for 27 FF-1s. No longer would there be a layoff because of a shortage of funds to pay the wages. In the depth of the Depression, Grumman had established itself as a planemaker to the Navy. To Boeing, Douglas and others, this was perhaps bad news; but to the Navy, to New York, and indeed to the United States, the name Grumman has ever since meant solid industrial strength with the very highest reputation in increasingly advanced technology.

The 27 FF-1s were all delivered in 1933, and from June of that year equipped fighter squadron VF-5B aboard USS *Lexington*. The slightly different SF-1 likewise received a production order, this time for 33, and these were delivered in the first half of 1934. Most of these went aboard the *Lexington* as well, with scouting squadron VS-3B. Their service career was highly satisfactory, and after withdrawal from first-line use in 1935–36 the 25 surviving Fifis were modified to FF-2 standard with dual pilot controls. Many, along with the SFs, survived in reserve squadrons up to World War II.

Above: Navy airplane No 9675 was one of the last of the main production run of F2F-1 fighters, powered by the slim 14-cylinder Twin Wasp Junior engine. It is seen serving with VF-2.

What next? It was pretty obvious, in retrospect. If the two-seat "Fert'l Myrt'l" could beat the single-seaters, what could a single-seat version do? Both Grumman and the Navy had the same idea, and initial drawings were submitted during the year at Valley Stream. This time, Grumman was an accepted contractor, and from the start the proposed single-seater was the XF2F-1. Naturally it came out as a smaller edition of the FF, but the big retracted wheels made the short and stumpy fuselage look even more pot-bellied. To improve the streamlining, Grumman picked the slim R-1535 engine, as proposed in the prototype XJF-1, with a long-chord cowl faired smoothly back into the fuselage. Currently the landplane speed record was held by a Gee Bee racer, whose big engine had the shortest possible body behind it. There was just a hint of this about the XF2F, but not so much as to give it the violently unsafe handling characteristics of the Gee Bee, which would have been unacceptable for carrier operation. In 1932 it was not easy to get high flight performance and also docile handling.

The Navy bought an XF2F-1 anyway, and on October 18, 1933, test pilot Paul Hovgard opened up the smooth 14-cylinder engine and took off from the Farmingdale grass. It proved to be a hot ship, indeed. The good news was that its speed range extended from a record 230 mph (370 km/h) down to a gentle 65 mph (105 km/h), while it could climb at an unprecedented 2,200 ft.min. The bad news was that it was as tricky as expected, and a stall (for example, in too tight a turn in the circuit) resulted in a sudden spin. Like the FF, it had an enclosed cockpit, though pilots often flew with the canopy slid back. Armament consisted of the usual two .30-caliber guns in the top of the fuselage, firing through the propeller disc.

After exhaustive testing by the customer, the Navy ordered no fewer than 55 production F2F-1s, the biggest single order it had placed since 1918. Coming on top of big orders for the FF, SF and JF, it meant that Grumman's workforce tripled in 1934 to a total of 207. Rather suddenly, and despite the Depression, Grumman had become a major Navy contractor and a major positive factor in the western Long Island economy. It also had to change the way it did things, moving across from "tin bashing" by hand to full-scale production methods with costly high-precision tooling, inspection departments, test laboratories, a wind tunnel and all the other state-of-the art equipment a big planemaker must have.

In January 1935 the fourth of the company's aircraft production lines started delivering F2Fs, which began a successful career equipping VF-2B aboard the carrier *Lexington* and VF-3B aboard the *Ranger*. The latter squadron became VF-7B aboard the *Yorktown* and then VF-5 embarked aboard the new *Wasp*, but it kept its rugged little "Flying Barrels" until 1939; VF-2B, the famous Fighting Two, kept them until 1940.

There is no doubt whatever that the F2F, Grumman's first single-seat fighter, represented a major step forward in aircraft design. Despite the penalties of being stressed for carrier operation, and fitted with sea flotation gear and other special equipment, it was so compact and neat that it could out perform any fighter in the Army Air Corps at the time, and – the author has no hesitation in claiming – any fighter in any of the world's air forces. A lot of this was due to the low aerodynamic drag, which in turn rested on the retractable landing gear (even the tailwheel folded away), the finely cowled engine and the well-streamlined fuselage with smooth metal skin. Drag was also reduced by the enclosed cockpit, which the Navy was fortunately able to introduce with all four of the new Grumman types without too much argument. In Europe, fighter pilots generally tried to prevent the introduction of cockpit canopies, claiming they had to lean out and look in all directions. They were able to do this only because their aircraft flew at less than 200 mph (322 km/h).

Below: The XSF-2, No 9493, was one-of-a-kind. It immediately followed the batch of SF-1s, and differed in having a Twin Wasp Junior and controllable Hamilton propeller. Note the extended gear and hook.

Good as it was, the F2F was not perfect. Before buying it in quantity, the Navy ordered the span to be slightly increased, the canopy enlarged and other details attended to. Despite the longer upper wing, the stability was still marginal in some conditions, and a few F2F's got into unintentional spins. Accordingly, Schwendler's growing design team came out with an improved model, the XF3F-1, and the Navy agreed that the last of the 55 fighters should be the first of the new version. To improve stability the wings were appreciably increased in span and the fuselage lengthened. The F2F cockpit was rather cramped, so in the XF3F it was made larger and more comfortable for big pilots.

Jimmy Collins flew the XF3F on March 20, 1935. It was clearly a real winner. Two days later the manufacturer's tests were being completed in a series of dives and pull-outs. On the very last dive the pilot was required to haul back on the stick so hard that, at the highest speed the aircraft could reach after a long almost vertical dive, the acceleration in the vertical plane would reach 9g, thus stressing the structure to nine times its normal loading. In fact, calculations showed that Collins pulled an unsurvivable 14g, and the speeding fighter broke up in the air, killing its pilot. This was the company's first real blow, but it quickly built a second XF3F with the same Navy serial number (9727). Almost unbelievably, during spinning trials at Anacostia, this machine

Below: A 1936 picture showing the new Farmingdale plant in full swing with the F3F-1. This was the last of the biplane fighters to have the R-1535 Twin Wasp Junior, seen being uncrated at left.

got into a spin from which no recovery appeared possible. Pilot Lee Gelbach parachuted to safety. The second 9727 was rebuilt in three weeks, and the spinning problem was cured by adding a small ventral fin under the fuselage tailcone.

Once this was done the Navy again had what was almost certainly the best fighter in the world. In August Grumman received a contract for 54 of the F3F-1s, which – not including the engines, guns and other GFE (Government-furnished equipment) – were priced at well over a million dollars. And, as before, Schwendler's team kept on cranking in improvements, the major one being a switch to a different engine. Though it had considerably greater diameter, making the fighter appear less streamlined, the big nine-cylinder Wright Cyclone had been developed to give an impressive 850 hp. Despite an increase in weight, the re-engined model promised to have significantly higher performance, partly because the Cyclone had a two-stage supercharger and swung a Hamilton propeller with three controllable-pitch blades. The Navy ordered a prototype (No 0452) with designation XF3F-2, and this performed so well that on March 23, 1937, the Navy placed an order for 81 F3F-2s priced at $1,674,310 for the lot - again, its biggest-ever aircraft contract.

Deliveries proceeded from July 1937 through May 1938, the new

Below: Another view of F3F-1 production, from the "finished" end of the line. Most of these fighters went to VF-5B and VF-6B, aboard *Ranger* and *Saratoga*.

Dash-2s going to VF-6 aboard USS *Enterprise* and two Marine squadrons, VMF-1 and VMF-2. Grumman's avalanche of work had increasingly caused it to subcontract work to other companies, and on the Dash-2 run the wings and tails were farmed out to Brewster Aeronautical Corporation in Long Island City. But there could never be too much work, and when Wright advised Grumman of the availability of an even more powerful Cyclone, the R-1820-22 with 950 hp, the 65th F3F-2 was pulled off the line and fitted with one of the new engines. This, too, went well with the Navy, and though in 1938 biplanes were becoming slightly passé, an order was quickly placed for 27 of the more powerful species, with the designation F3F-3. Delivered between December 1938 and May 1939, they replaced the F2F's of squadron VF-5. They were the last biplane fighters ordered for any U.S. service, and they were bought simply because Grumman delivered everything the biplane design had to offer.

During the late 1930s the JF family produced steady income, and brought the company its first export orders (from Argentina). North of the border, the Canadian Car & Foundry Company decided in 1937 to enter what seemed to be a growing industry and obtained a license to build the old FF-1. What made this interesting is that, in addition to 15 for the RCAF, CanCar delivered 40 for what it thought was a Turkish customer, but which really went to the Spanish Republicans, who

became the first customer to go to war with Grumman products.

Another rather unexpected customer was the Gulf Oil Company. For many years this giant had gained great publicity by sending one of the most famed pilots, Major Al (Alford) Williams, around the country to give quite unbelievable aerobatic displays. In 1936 he came to Grumman to see if the Cyclone-powered F3F might be a good choice as a replacement for the Curtiss Gulfhawk he was using. After wringing out a production model – which made the management nervous, not least because it belonged to the Navy – Williams said it was the most responsive ship he had ever flown. The result was the Grumman G-22 Gulfhawk II, a really hot ship with an F3F fuselage (without ventral fin), F2F wings and a Cyclone rated at 1,000 hp. Maximum speed was

Left: Distinguished by its two-place cockpit, the G-32A (company construction number 477) was a demonstrator retained by the company and often flown by Mr. Grumman himself. Here it has been repainted as a Navy ship with number 0447 and squadron insignia.

Left: Fastest of all the Grumman biplanes, the G-22 Gulfhawk II was one of a series of special aerobatic demonstrators built for Gulf Oil and flown by the famed Maj. Al Williams. Capable of 290 290mph. (467 km/h), and of flying inverted for 30 minutes, it proudly resides today in the National Air & Space Museum, Washington, D.C.

Designation: G-21A GOOSE.
Type: Multi-role amphibian.
Powerplant: Two Pratt & Whitney R-985 Wasp Junior radial engines, 450 hp.
Wingspan: 49 ft 0 in.
Length: 38 ft 4 in.
Height: 15 ft 0 in.
Weight: 5,425 lb; later 8,000 lb.
Maximum Speed: 210 mph.
Ceiling: 21,000 ft.
Range: 640 miles.
Armament: None
Crew: 2 pilots, plus accommodation for up to 8 passengers.
Users: Portugal, RAF, RCAF, USAAF, USCG.

Below: Roy Grumman and Jake Swirbul with a G-44 executive amphibian.

290 mph (467 km/h), and in its shiny eye-catching orange-red color scheme it thrilled spectators throughout North America and Europe.

By this time America was beginning to pull out from the Great Depression, but for Grumman this had been a period of amazing success. It had done almost everything right, not least in aiming its operations squarely at the Navy instead of the shaky civil market. But there had been times when a broadening of the market base had seemed sensible, and from time to time the top men had recalled their work on the Loening Air Yachts, a small series of amphibians seating up to seven and aimed at the wealthy playboy and emerging corporate markets. These had had a single pusher engine, but it seemed that, provided wing-mounted engines could be placed high enough to avoid waves and spray, a twin-engine design would be better, with a conventional flying-boat hull. It so happened that in 1936 some of the most famous and wealthy businessmen got together to consider having just such an airplane built, and the result was the G-21 Goose.

Grumman's biggest design so far, and utterly unlike its compact biplanes, it was a high-wing monoplane with a deep boat-type hull, twin 400-hp Pratt & Whitney Wasp Junior engines and stabilizing floats near the wingtips. The main landing wheels could be cranked up into recesses in the sides of the hull, and the tailwheel retracted as well. A door on the left, just behind the wing, led straight into the cabin, which could seat up to eight. Ahead was the two-place cockpit. Altogether it was a most attractive machine and a true forerunner of today's executive jets; Grumman decided to build three. The first was flown on May 29, 1937, and performed beyond all expectations, among other things reaching 201 mph (323 km/h). Still bothered by the risk, the company produced another seven Gooses, but it need not have worried. The cabin could be used to carry generals or admirals, or litter patients, or trainee navigators or radio operators, or a photo crew, or many other loads. It could even tow targets. Soon the Army adopted it as the OA-9, buying 27. Portugal bought 12 without landing gear but with guns and bombs. The biggest customer of all was the Navy Coast Guard, which called the Goose the JRF, and when the last one went out the door in World War II it was the 345th off the line!

Though strictly a product of the next decade, Grumman was so encouraged by the Goose, it produced a smaller version - the G-44 Widgeon, which began flight tests on June 28, 1940. Powered by two 200-hp Ranger six-cylinder in-line engines driving the now rare fixed-pitch wooden propellers, the Widgeon was aimed at a large market that could not afford the Goose. Typically with seats for two in the cockpit and three of four in the cabin, the Widgeon repeated the story of the Goose, selling to civil customers, to foreign air forces, to the Army, Navy and Coast Guard, and to Britain, which applied the more appropriate name of Gosling. Well over 300 were built, including 30 made under license in France after World War II.

Back in 1936 it had become evident that not even the Farmingdale factory could accommodate all the work, and a totally new plant, this time designed to Grumman's requirements, was built a few miles away at Bethpage, alongside the Long Island Railroad. Construction began in October 1936, and Grumman moved in on April 8, 1937. By this time the company could see what its next Navy fighter would look like.

Design of what obviously would be the XF4F-1 began in early 1936, as a slightly smaller and faster F3F. But the Navy bought a new monoplane fighter from Brewster, and Grumman knew it had to give up biplanes. It was a case of "back to the drawing board" and in July 1936 the Navy placed an order for an XF4F-2 (No. 0383). It was a completely new design, though it retained the tubby barrel-like fuselage with landing gears tucked up into it behind the engine. In the front was Pratt & Whitney's new R-1830 Twin Wasp 14-cylinder engine, conservatively rated at 900 hp. Amidships were rather rounded wings, located mid-high on the round fuselage. The enclosed cockpit, well positioned above the wing, gave the pilot an excellent view. As on the later F3F's the two guns positioned in the fuselage ahead of the pilot were of hard-hitting .50-caliber, and two 100-lb bombs could be hung under the wings.

Below: The Goose was the first of Grumman's many "executive" airplanes. A trim amphibian, it saw wide wartime use, though this example with British markings has a U.S. experimental civil registration.

Bottom: A 1942 photograph of a J4F-1 (G-44 Widgeon) of the U.S. Coast Guard on anti-submarine patrol with a 100-lb bomb.

There were a number of innovations. The complete wing, which was of very generous area—232 sq ft (21.55 m²)—in order to achieve the necessary good turn radius and slow landing speed for carrier operation, was made entirely of stressed metal for greater strength and to stand up to harsh service use. It had a new NACA profile, and under its trailing edge were split-type landing flaps. No hydraulic system was fitted, the flaps being worked by a vacuum system and the pilot cranked up the landing gear by hand.

Bob Hall, designer of the Gee Bee racer and a gifted engineer, was test pilot on the XF4F's first flight, from the new Bethpage field, on September 2, 1937. From the start Grumman knew they had another winner, but the new Pratt & Whitney engine caused prolonged and severe problems. In 1939 the French, for quite different reasons, insisted on using the Wright Cyclone; had this engine been installed from the start, Grumman might have gotten the F4F into production at least 18 months sooner. As it was, the Navy had little option but to buy the generally inferior Brewster F2A, but it always wanted a new-generation Grumman and kept the company's prototype development funded.

In October 1938 an order was placed for an XF4F-3 with bigger wings of 260 sq ft (24.15m²) area, revised tail surfaces and an R-1830-

Below: Looking down into the cockpit of the first monoplane fighter, the XF4F-2. The big handle on the right cranked the landing gear.

Below right: The one and only XF4F-2, first of the Wildcats. Armed with two .50-caliber machine guns in the fuselage and two 100-lb bombs (which are fitted), it crashed out of fuel and was rebuilt as the first XF4F-3.

76 Twin Wasp engine with a two-stage two-speed supercharger that produced 1,050 hp and much greater power at high altitude. New armament included two .30-caliber guns in the fuselage and two .50 in the outer wings. Though considerably heavier than the Dash-2, this aircraft reached an excellent 333 mph (536 km/h) and showed impressive maneuverability, as well as a service ceiling of 33,500 ft. First flown on February 12, 1939, the Dash-3 showed that the bigger problems were solved, and at last, in August 1939, just before the start of World War II, the Navy felt it could order 54 of the new fighters. Clearly, in view of the massive and growing need for warplanes, this was just for starters. The production F4F-3 had a longer fuselage and heavier armament of four .50-caliber guns in the huge outer wings. The F4F-3 had shortcomings, but they were matters of detail, concerning such things as engine cooling, cockpit ventilation and the addition of armor and self-sealing tanks. The important thing was that here was the next Grumman fighter, though nobody then knew how vitally important it would be.

Yet, before the 1930s ended, Grumman had designed a totally

different fighter that would make the F4F obsolate. In close partnership with the Navy, and assisted by Wright and the NACA, the company began in 1938 to design a fighter that can fairly be called futuristic. The one thing that looked normal was the wing, of stressed-skin construction and with the outer panels folding straight up and over to halve the normal span of 42 ft for carrier storage. In front of the wing jutted the two massive Cyclone engines – special XR-1820s, each putting out 1,200 hp and driving the new Curtiss constant-speed propellers. At the back was the short fuselage, the nose of which stopped at the main spar of the wing, with a twin-fin tail. Because of the predicted performance, the Navy ordered a prototype, the XF5F-1, known to Grumman as the G-34 Skyrocket. The name was appropriate enough, because when Bud Gillies flew the beast on April 1, 1940, it could be seen to climb at an unprecedented 4,000 ft (1,219 m) per minute, besides travelling on the level at 383 mph (616 km/h).

Planned to be armed with two massive 23mm Madsen cannons and a light bomb load, the XF5F was certainly a fantastic performer, but it had problems. Stability was marginal, view on carrier approach could be obstructed by the nacelles, the engines overheated, and in any case this would have been a very large step up in power and performance aboard carriers. The nose was lengthened, an arrester hook fitted

Below: A fabulous picture of the one and only XF5F-1 Skyrocket, a carrier-based fighter prototype of amazing capability which perhaps was way ahead of its time.

and many other changes were made. But the increased weight and high price tag were too much for Grumman and the Navy to swallow. From airfields, however, such a fighter presented fewer problems. In November 1939 a revised model, the G-46, was offered to the Army Air Corps. There was immediate interest, and an order for a prototype, the XP-50. This took some time to build, because Grumman was working around the clock on an overload of other work. But when Bob Hall at last took the aircraft into the air on February 18, 1941, it had a non-folding wing, much bigger fuselage of beautiful streamline form, turbocharged R-1820 engines and a tricycle landing gear. The estimated maximum speed was no less than 427 mph (687 km/h) at 25,000 feet (7,600 m).

But the aircraft's capabilities were never fully realized because of an accident that occured during a test flight on May 14, 1941. Bob Hall had the XP-50 in a steep climb at almost full power when one engine's turbocharger failed violently and severed the landing gear hydraulic lines. The airplane was still flyable with one engine and Hall managed to lower one main landing gear, but the nose wheel would not come down even when Hall applied additional pressure from an emergency air bottle.

The Army XP-50 had an estimated speed and ceiling of 427 mph (687 km/h) and 40,000 ft (12,192m) and enormous potential.

With the aircraft in this condition, attempting an emergency landing was out of the question. But rather than bail out and risk being hit by the tail, Hall climbed out of the cockpit, slid along the turtle-back of the fuselage and dropped off from between the vertical tails.

He was picked up out of Long Island Sound and the airplane crashed into the water north of Eaton's Neck.

A small boy on City Island beach who was watching the high-flying XP-50, noticed the smoke from the damaged engine and, a minute or so later, saw a splash as something hit the water close by. He fished the object out and it proved to be one of the turbochargers assembled with bolts made of the wrong metal. The two halves of the wheel had pulled slightly apart and the blades (buckets) had separated, the fragments cutting the hydraulic lines.

Despite this, the Army's interest remained strong. Could Grumman build another XP-50? Swirbul replied they were so busy they could not consider it unless the Army could assure subsequent production of 1,000. He knew no such assurance could be given, and throughout the coming war Grumman was to build for the Navy and not the Army. This was not exactly a handicap. Every one of the company's resources was about to be stretched to the limits.

The Sky's the Limit

Previous Page: "The Grumman Wildcat it is no exaggeration to say, did more than any single instrument of war to save the day for the United States in the Pacific," wrote Foster Hailey, New York Times Correspondent, 1943.

Below: In 1941 Navy airplanes were often camouflaged overall light gray, very like today's low visibility camouflage. This F4F-3, with non-folding wings, served Marine fighter squadron VMF-121.

Bottom: Probably assigned to VF-4 (USS *Ranger*), this F4F-3 was one of the first F4F's accepted by the Navy in 1940. The extra insignia ahead of the wing was the "Neutrality Star."

Grumman opened its second decade with a staggering amount of work. Just one product, the F4F Wildcat carrier-based fighter, promised business that could possibly outstrip the company's manufacturing potential, despite the unchecked growth in manpower and plant floor area throughout the 1930s. An important part of the market for the F4F looked likely to be foreign. During the 1930s Grumman had flourished on repeated contracts from the U.S. Navy. Except for Germany, European and other governments had soft-pedalled defense hardware, and in any case supported their own industries. Now, suddenly, the nations of Europe were desperately trying to arm themselves, and the United States was the obvious big and capable offshore armament source.

During the period of growing tension in Europe at the end of the 1930s, the U.S. Government had tried to remain detached, and there was a strong and understandable isolationist feeling. Once the war had actually begun, such a belief appeared unreal if not perilous, and the Roosevelt administration unhesitatingly authorized colossal increases in arms production. Thus, while in 1939 the Navy had placed orders for just 78 of the original F4F-3 Wildcat, total F4F orders for 1940

amounted to 759 – and even this was just for starters.

Clearly, an expansion of war production potential on an unprecedented scale was needed, and quickly. Congress passed the Emergency Plant Facilities Act, providing for the construction at government expense of enormous facilities for the production of war material, the plants being occupied and run by existing defense contractors but remaining government property. One of the very first such contracts provided a building that became Grumman's Plant 2. It was located on the other side of the growing runway from the original site, which became Plant 1. From the start Plant 2 was a giant, but during World War II it was to be extended until the total new floor area at Bethpage amounted to 2,650,000 sq ft (246,193 m²), or about 61 acres.

More than any other U.S. aircraft company, Grumman was to concentrate its wartime effort at one site, Bethpage, building aircraft chiefly for one customer, the U.S. Navy. Grumman's performance was to be outstanding.

The original wartime product, the F4F-3, was perfect in many respects. A serious shortcoming, though, was that its wings did not fold, and because they stuck out much further than the compact biplane

Below: By 1940 the Bethpage plant, later called Plant 1, had begun to expand. Here the first extension can be seen at the left end. Parked in front of it are a Goose and a Duck, and out on the field is a visiting Navy staff transport (stagger-wing Beech).

Above: Mr. Grumman demonstrating his conception of the "stowing" using paper clips and a rubber eraser.

wings of Grumman's previous fighters this became a significant problem. By 1940 the Navy was beginning to think in terms of large numbers of small escort carriers – CVE's – to which the new F4F was almost ideally suited, except for its large dimensions that took up so much shipboard space. In 1940 Mr. Grumman himself put his mind to work on the problem. It would have been quite simple just to design wings that would hinge upwards, as in some other naval aircraft. But he thought this design would be structurally undesirable, besides making the folded aircraft very tall and laterally unstable on a rolling deck. Birds can fold their wings back alongside their bodies, and this seemed a better arrangement. He saw that, by attaching the folding outer portions of the wing with skewed-axis hinges, they could be made to pivot around to the rear while simultaneously rotating to be stowed leading edge down. Besides saving space the skewed-axis design would prevent the wings from folding in flight. Mr. Grumman picked up two paperclips and unbent two of the ends to stick out at an angle. These he stuck into opposite sides of an eraser, to represent the folding wings. After some trial and error he had a perfect pair of "wings" folding in exactly the way he had envisaged.

In 1940 this was no more than an idea. It had to be translated into detailed engineering drawings, built, tested, and finally brought in on the production line. The intense and mounting pressure for more and more F4Fs made all this doubly difficult. This pressure naturally arose from the fact that, after a few early problems, the F4F-3 developed into an exceptionally fine airplane. Its unique square-tip wings and overall design made it one of the most maneuverable monoplane fighters in the sky, even in mock dogfights with rival land-based fighters which could use big airfields and were not encumbered by aircraft carrier arresting gear. With either the Pratt & Whitney R-1830 engine, as selected by the U.S. Navy, or the Wright R-1820 as picked by France, the maximum speed was an excellent 335 mph (539 km/h) at medium to high altitudes, and the initial rate of climb possibly set a new record for fighters at

3,100 ft/min (15.7m/sec). This was despite a considerable increase in firepower. The original armament of two .30-caliber fuselage guns and two .50-caliber guns in the wings was replaced by four of the larger size, all in the wings. Another important change was the addition of cockpit armor and strengthening of the landing gear so that it could withstand the harshest treatment aboard any carrier.

These changes took time to implement, so that in fact the first F4F-3 delivery was to the British Fleet Air Arm. The British had not originally ordered the Grumman fighter, but quickly took over the French order for 81 when France fell in June 1940. The French machines, called G-36A's, had numerous Gallic features, such as metric instruments and a throttle lever which operated backwards, but these were all modified to meet British requirements before the first aircraft was handed over on July 27, 1940. The British called the aircraft the Martlet, the heraldic name for a martin or swallow. It had non-folding wings and was therefore based ashore. The first squadron equipped was No. 804, at Hatston in the Orkney Islands, north of Scotland. On Christmas Day 1940, two of 804s Marlet Is were vectored by ground radar to intercept a Ju 88 and shot it down, scoring the first combat victory for a Grumman airplane and the first by a U.S. aircraft in British service.

Designation: F4F WILDCAT.
Type: Fighter.
Powerplant: Pratt & Whitney R-1830-76 Twin Wasp. 14-cylinder radial, air cooled, 1,200 hp; later (FM-2) Wright R-1820 Cyclone, 1,350 hp.
Wingspan: 38 ft 0 in.
Length: 28 ft 9 in.
Height: 11 ft 0 in.
Weight: 7,952 lb; later 8,271 lb.
Maximum Speed: 318 mph; FM-2 332 mph.
Ceiling: 34,900 ft.
Range: 845 miles.
Armament: 6 x 0.5-in machine guns; 200 lb of bombs.
Crew: 1.
Users: RCAF, RN, USMC, USN.

Left above: The first of the G-36 monoplane family to go into action were Martlets of Britain's Fleet Air Arm (later the name was changed to the U.S. name, Wildcat). This Wildcat V of FAA No. 882 Sqn is about to take off from the small escort carrier HMS *Searcher*.

Left: Grumman ingenuity and engineering skill was made evident by the sto-wing. Here the wing's advantage is emphasized in a "five into two" demonstration using F4F-4s.

In the summer of 1940 Grumman was busy with many experimental engine installations in the F4F-3. Many other improvements were also being developed – some as the result of combat experience in Europe, such as self sealing gas tanks. Though a U.S. Navy F4F-3 had flown in February 1940, the first fully modified aircraft for inventory service flew on August 20, 1940. It was powered by an R-1830-76 rated for takeoff at 1,200 hp. Deliveries to squadron VF-41 on December 4, 1940, were quickly followed by others to VF-7. The Navy was still unhappy with the two-stage R-1830 engine, and in November 1940 an XF4F-6 was flown with a single-stage version. This was ordered into production as the F4F-3A, but the first 30 were diverted under the new Lend-Lease Act to Greece, which had been invaded. That country was overrun by the Germans while the 30 aircraft were still at Gilbraltar, so they were switched to Britain as Martlet IIIs. Other Dash-3A's went to the Marine Corps.

Grumman's typical policy on the folding wing was to make absolutely certain that it worked perfectly before committing it to production. Eventually it was agreed to bring it in with the 163rd aircraft, at the same time adding two further guns in the outer wings to increase the formidable armament to six .50-caliber guns. Powered by the 1,200-hp R-1830-86, the new model was called the F4F-4, or in the Fleet Air Arm the Martlet II. Quickly embarked in British escort carrier HMS *Audacity*, Mk II aircraft of 802 Squadron shot down a giant Fw 200C Condor on September 20, 1941. On this carrier's second voyage they shot down four more, at last getting the measure of the aircraft Prime Minister Churchill called "the scourge of the Atlantic."

When Japan attacked Pearl Harbor on December 7, 1941, Marine squadron VMF-211 lost nine F4F-3s on the ground, and another seven at Wake Island on the following day. But the four battered survivors at Wake fought on under the most impossible conditions until the last was destroyed an amazing two weeks later. In those two weeks they destroyed a bomber, a destroyer and a transport ship. In subsequent actions throughout the Pacific the stout Grumman fighter was for all practical purposes the only Allied fighter to be effective in contesting command of the sky against the massed Japanese armadas. By far the most important version was the F4F-4, the mount of such famed aces as Lt. Cmdr. John S. Thach of VF-3, Lt. Butch O'Hare (after whom Chicago's main airport is named) of VF-42, Marine Maj. John L. Smith and Capt. Marion Carl of VMF-223.

Grumman completed the 1,971st and last F4F-4 on the last day of 1942. But the greatest possible number of F4F's – officially named Wildcat in October 1941 - were still needed. General Motors had unused auto plants along the East Coast, and in January 1942 formed Eastern Aircraft Division to put these to work building Grumman airplanes under license. The Linden, New Jersey, plant completed its first FM-1 from Grumman parts in August, 1942. This version being basically an F4F-4 with only four guns but more ammunition. Eastern produced 839 FM-1s. Biggest production of all (4,437) was the FM-2, with the 1,350-hp R-1820-56 Cyclone and a taller tail. From No. 3,301, the FM-2s also carried six 5-inch (127-mm) rockets under the wings. Excluding prototypes, a combined total of 7,898 F4F's and FM's of all versions were produced.

While the F4F was essentially the Navy's only operational fighter until the end of August 1943, when Grumman's own F6F went into action, the company also produced the Navy's standard carrier-based torpedo bomber of World War II. At the time of Pearl Harbor this mission was being flown by the Douglas TBD, an aircraft that soon showed it could not survive in combat against the Japanese. As early as 1939 the Navy had considered a successor, and a specification was issued at the start of 1940. It demanded tough numerical values for speed and mission radius while carrying the 21.7-inch (55cm) long Mk 13-2 short air torpedo or a 2,000-lb. (907-kg) bomb load. Clearly, thanks to the development by Pratt & Whitney and Wright of new high-power engines, it would be possible to produce an aircraft far superior to the TBD, but what the Navy wanted was the best it could get – of course! A team under Bob Hall quickly created a masterpiece in design which was to give the company its second giant war-winning product. Designated TBF and ultimately named Avenger, it was picked over rivals on April 8, 1940, and the first of two prototypes was flown by Hall on August 7, 1941.

A typically sturdy Grumman all-metal aircraft, the TBF was one of the biggest and heaviest aircraft ever designed for carrier operation

Above: The famed Butch O'Hare, about to fly a mission at Tarawa in 1943.

Below: An immaculate hangar deck full of F4F-4s aboard the escort carrier USS *Charger* (CVE-30) in October 1942.

Main picture: Deck crews sprint to unhook a landed TBF and fold its wings. The wings were big, and folding the wings was quite a job on a rolling ship in a high wind.

Inset: Readied for catapulting, a radar-equipped TBF-1C runs up its big 14-cylinder Cyclone R-2600 to full power. The prong on the wingtip is the pitot tube.

up, to that time. Wing area was 490 sq.ft. (45.52 m^2), and the empty weight – over 10,000 lb. (4,545 kg) in the first version, and more later – was almost half as much again as the loaded weight of an F4F. In the front was a Wright R-2600 double-row Cyclone engine putting out 1,700 hp. But this was lost in a fuselage so capacious that some Navy men called the big bird The Pregnant Beast, or even The Turkey (but a turkey it certainly was not). Perched high on top was the pilot, equipped with a .30-caliber gun firing ahead. Under the wing was a large internal bay, with hydraulically operated folding doors, for a torpedo, mine, bombs of up to 2,000 lb. (907 kg), or a tank of auxiliary fuel or smokescreen liquid. Aft of the wing on the right was a door admitting to a rear compartment packed with equipment and also provided with a seat for the bombardier, who could face forward to aim bombs (the pilot aimed the aircraft in torpedo attacks) or face aft and man a defensive machine gun covering the underside of the tail – a completely new feature for carrier-based aircraft. Even more remarkable was that, instead of the traditional rear cockpit with a hand-aimed gun, the upper rear defense was provided by a .50-caliber gun aimed with precision by a power-driven enclosed rotary turret. Synchronized electric motors with amplidyne generator control gave fingertip accuracy to the gunner, even with the TBF at full throttle at up to 278 mph (447 km/h).

Above: One of the first photographs ever taken of a formation of TBF's in mid-1942.

Above: Trundling a 21.7-in "tin fish" to a waiting TBM for a strike against the Japanese fleet off Cape Engaro during the Battle of Leyte Gulf in October 1944. The TBM was the TBF made by Eastern Aircraft.

It added up to everything the Navy had come to expect from Grumman, and in December 1940 a massive order was placed for 286 TBF's off the drawing board.

Construction work went on round the clock to complete Plant 2 where Grumman would build the TBF. On the unseasonably warm Sunday morning of December 7, 1941, almost every Grumman employee was present with his family as Plant 2 was dedicated. Spotlighted on the vast production floor was the second XTBF. Then Clint Towl was called to the telephone. He was told Japan had struck at Pearl Harbor. Imperceptibly, with no broadcast announcement, the festivities were brought to a conclusion. When the last visitor had left, the gates were locked and the entire Bethpage complex searched for saboteurs. Grumman remained a secure place throughout the war, and after, while growing to a size never dreamed of.

The first production TBF-1 flew on January 3, 1942. From the start everyone knew it was a winner, and despite its size it could cut through the sky with such determination that quite soon the .30-caliber gun above the engine was replaced by two punchy "fifties" in the wings. Soon the British invention of airborne radar was added, either a Westinghouse ASB or an APS-4 set in a pod hung under the right wing. wing. Britain's Fleet Air Arm received 395 slightly modified Avengers, far superior to the homegrown Barracuda, while with the help of GM's Eastern Aircraft Division no fewer than 9,939 Avengers rolled off the wartime production lines. All were basically just like the No. 1 aircraft, though most had underwing racks for rockets or drop tanks. A few pioneered the totally new technique of carrying aloft a giant airborne surveillance radar, a field in which Grumman was later to excel.

Above: An Avenger AS.4, supplied under the MDAP program to Britain's Fleet Air Arm in the 1950s, catches a wire; the ship is probably HMS *Illustrious* and the squadron No. 815.

Left: Avenger Is of the Fleet Air Arm No. 852 Sqn (HMS *Nabob*) on convoy escort in 1944.

Designation: TBF-1 AVENGER.
Type: Torpedo Bomber.
Powerplant: Wright R-2600-8 Cyclone, 14-cylinder. Radial, air-cooled, 1,700 hp.
Wingspan: 54 ft 2 in.
Length: 40 ft 0 in.
Height: 16 ft 5 in.
Weight: 15,905 lb; later 17,895 lb.
Maximum Speed: 271 mph at 12,000 ft.
Ceiling: 22,400.
Range: 1,215 miles.
Armament: 1 x 0.5-in and 2 x 3-in machine guns; 1,600 lb of Torpedoes or Bombs.
Crew: 3.
Users: RN, RNZAF, USN; many other post-war.

Above: "Rosie the riveter" helped win WW II.

Below: TBF's and (right) F6F's aboard CVE-26 *Monterey*, probably off Okinawa in the late fall of 1944.

In World War II the Avenger was by far the Allies' most important naval torpedo bomber, and it racked up a tremendous combat record against the Japanese fleets in the Pacific and against Hitler's U-boats in the Atlantic. In the 1950s, greatly modified Avengers served in the ASW (anti-submarine warfare) role, as well as the new duty of radar picket with a giant "Guppy" radome under the belly. Nobody at the time of Pearl Harbor would have believed that the last nation to operate this great aircraft would be Japan!

So great was the contribution to Allied victory made by the F4F and TBF that it seems almost beyond belief that neither was Grumman's No. 1 wartime product. This honor went to a completely new fighter, the F6F Hellcat; and this one type of airplane did far more to win the war of the Pacific than all other aircraft combined.

Long before Pearl Harbor, Grumman designers had been studying and drawing improved versions of the F4F. The most basic demand was a much more powerful engine, either a Wright R-2600 Cyclone or the even more potent Pratt & Whitney R-2800 Double Wasp. The airframe was redesigned to have a bigger fuselage with a cross-section more pear-shaped than circular, with the pilot high above the wing. The wing remained chunky and squarish, with the same neat sto-wing folding arrangement, but the main landing gears were completely different. As in the TBF, the legs were hinged to the outer end of the fixed wing center section, giving a track much wider than that of the F4F, for better stability on deck. The TBF gears folded outwards, but on the F6F they folded to the rear, the wheels rotating 90^0 to lie flat in

Top left: Few airplanes have ever been built so fast or so efficiently as the F6F's.

Top: By 1944 approximately onethird of the line workers on the F6F were female.

the wing immediately ahead of the slotted flaps. The masssive engine was neatly installed, with ducts for the oil cooler and supercharger intercooler inside the lower part of the cowling. Fuel was housed in self-sealing tanks under the cockpit floor and between the center-section wing spars. Armament comprised six powerful .50-caliber guns in tight groups in the outer wings, and there was provision for a centerline drop tank or various bombs, weighing up to 2,000 lb. (907 kg), or six of the new 5-inch (127-mm) HVAR's (high-velocity aircraft rockets).

Bob Hall flew the prototype XF6F-1 on June 26, 1942, the engine being the R-2600 as in the TBF. A totally new Plant 3 was already beginning to take shape at Bethpage specifically to build the new F6F, which looked to be the most important combat aircraft ever bought by the Navy. And, unlike Grumman's other great war winners, the F6F was to be made by Grumman alone. Though the company opened a few smaller facilities on Long Island, it was the great Bethpage complex that really produced the Hellcat, and produced it in impressive numbers in a very short time. The second of the two XF6F's, BuNo 02982, was powered by the bigger 2,000 hp R-2800-10 engine, and flown on July 30, 1942. It was a remarkable achievement to fly the second airplane only a month behind the first. It had a totally different engine, but the same good balance and flight control.

In fact the F6F never needed much modification, and the main problem was how to get it into production fast enough. Grumman bought thousands of steel girders from the New York elevated railroad and from the World's Fair, quickly riveting them into Plant 3. Despite this, the detailed jigging and tooling for the F6F tended to run ahead of the factory. Main-gear fairings were simplified, the engine inclination was altered for minimum drag at maximum speed (so that in most flight conditions the thrust line was horizontal and the main fuselage was tilted tail-down), and the propeller was changed from a spinnered Curtiss to a Hamilton Hydromatic with no spinner. Production then

Above: A pair of F6F-5 Hellcats flying from Floyd Bennet Field over New York City with the U.S. Naval Reserves after the war.

Designation: F6F-3 HELLCAT.
Type: Fighter.
Powerplant: Pratt & Whitney R2800-10 Double Wasp 18-cylinder radial, air cooled, 2,000 hp.
Wingspan: 42 ft 10 in.
Length: 33 ft 7 in.
Height: 13 ft 1 in.
Weight: 15,413 lb.
Maximum Speed: 376 mph.
Ceiling: 38,400 ft.
Range: 1,090 miles.
Armament: 6 x 0.5-in machine guns; F6F-5 also 2,000 lb of bombs or rockets.
Crew: 1.
Users: RN,USMC, USN.

rolled, and for starters Bethpage turned out 4,403 F6F-3s, including 18 converted as F6F-3E night fighters with an APS-4 radar pod under the starboard wing, and 205 F6F-3N night fighters with the APS-6 radar in the same location, as well as a 2,200-hp R-2800-10W with water injection and a flat bulletproof windshield. Hellcat production was completed by delivering 7,870 F6F-5s with an improved airframe with spring-tab ailerons and other small improvements; some late Dash-5s had two 20-mm cannons and four .50 caliber guns. The overall production figure included 1,529 F6F-5N night fighters and about 200 camera-equipped F6F-5P reconnaissance conversions.

In addition to the U.S. Navy, the F6F was supplied in considerable numbers to the British Fleet Air Arm, at first called the Gannet, but later given the U.S. name to avoid confusion. As in the case of the Wildcat and Avenger, the Grumman product was so markedly superior that the Fleet Air Arm received 252 F6F-3s (Hellcat I), 930 F6F-5s (Hellcat II) and 80 F6F-5N's (Hellcat NF.II night fighters). Some Mk IIs were fitted with cameras as FR.IIs and others had guns removed to become dedicated PR.II reconnaissance aircraft.

The Bethpage plants delivered no fewer than 12,275 F6F's in just 30 months in 1943–45. The F6F-3 went into action with VF-5, operating from the *Yorktown* in the second strike on Marcus Island on August 31, 1943. Right from the start the F6F was what everyone in the Pacific theater had been praying for: the fighter to beat the Zero. In the first big battle, in the Kwajalein/Roi area on December 4, 1943, 91 F6F's met 50 A6M Zeros and destroyed 28 for the loss of two. By the end of the war the F6F had destroyed a confirmed 5,155 out of the U.S. Navy's total carrier-based score of 6,477. This is all the more remarkable when it is realized the F6F was in action for less than two years.

It is hard to think of any program in history for a combat airplane that was so timely, so absolutely right from the start, built in such numbers

Left: An F6F-3 bearing six "kill" flags is readied for takeoff from *Lexington* during the Marianas strikes in 1944 (in the backround is *North Carolina*).

Below: Launch of an F6F of VF-1 "Top Hatters" during the same Marianas Turkey Shoot of June 1944; the ship is *Yorktown*.

Bottom: Gear comes up as an F6F leaves CVL 26 *Monterey* for the raid on Okinawa on October 10, 1944.

Above: One of the very first F6F's in 1942 livery. Deliveries began in 1943.

Right: An F6F-3 on carrier qualification trials in the early summer of 1943 about to make a free takeoff.

with such speed by a single company, and used in a shooting war to such tremendous effect. Despite the presence of the Wildcat, until August 1943 the Japanese had the better of the air war over a very large portion of the Earth's surface, making it difficult for the Allies to push back the enemy's land and sea forces. After August 1943, mainly because of the Hellcat, the tables were turned absolutely, and the tough, powerful Grumman fighters not only dominated the sky but also made life perilous for the Japanese invaders wherever they were to be found.

Yet, remarkably, the F6F was by no means Grumman's fastest or most powerful fighter developed during World War II. Back in early 1941 the Navy was building the first of the great 45,000-ton Midway class carriers, and these could operate aircraft of unprecedented size, weight and power. On the last day of Fiscal Year 1941, two prototypes were ordered of the XF7F-1 Tigercat, a formidable machine which, though a single-seat fighter, had 4,000 horsepower from two massive R-2800 (Hellcat-type) engines. Other unprecedented features for a naval fighter were a tricycle landing gear and armament of four 20-mm cannon and four .50-caliber machine guns, as well as a torpedo or heavy bomb load. Without offensive stores it could fly at 425 mph (684 km/h). Range, rate of climb and many other aspects of performance promised to set new records.

Above: One of the first photographs of a production F6F Hellcat, showing the red-bordered insignia in use during July and August 1943.

Grumman turned out 34 F7F-1 day fighters, 66 two-seat F7F-2N night fighters with radar replacing the .50 caliber guns, 250 F7F-3s with increased fuel capacity and a larger fin (60 completed as two-seat 3N night fighters with a very long nose and a radome on its underside), and finally a dozen F7F-4N's with even better radar and structural improvements. Grumman delivered the F7F-3s with the provision for them to be either 3N's or 3P's. Lockheed Air Service did the conversions for the Navy. The Tigercat first flew on December 2, 1943, and was a great airplane, serving primarily ashore with the Marines. In Korea the -3N's and a few -3P's (converted for the photo-recon mission) put up a fine record. At least two F7F's are still flying.

The F7F was a large, heavy aircraft not ideally suited for carriers (there were some who thought even the F6F a trifle big) and after carefully studying 18 months of information concerning air combat from the carriers, Grumman designed the F8F, a totally new fighter that was smaller and 2,000 lbs. lighter than the F6F and one of the most compact machines of its time, despite being powered by the same chunky and powerful R-2800 Double Wasp engine. The engine turned a big four-blade propeller, and the result was a fighter that had few rivals for speed, quick takeoff, rate and angle of climb, and all-round combat maneuverability. Two prototypes were ordered on November 27, 1943, and the first flew on August 31, 1944. The F8F could be called an engine with a saddle on it. The center of gravity was eight inches ahead of the engine firewall. The top of the aircraft's one-piece wing formed the floor of the cockpit, and the pilot sat on a sheet of metal attached to a structure above the wing. By adding his own personalized cushion, the pilot raised himself high enough to see out of the cockpit. A big man had to sit a little sideways to fit between the cockpit side rails.

One innovation tested on some of the early models was a breakaway wing tip. The tips were blown off by explosive charges actuated by sensing devices. If the pilot exceeded 8.5g, the outer three feet of each wing would break off preventing a catastrophic failure of the entire wing. But because the wing tips could not be made to break off simultaneously, the innovation was removed from the test aircraft and never incorporated into other F8F's. One of the acid tests of a planemaker is the time taken to go from prototype to production, during which hundreds of bugs have to be sorted out to the customer's satisfaction. Grumman had set an astounding pace with the F6F, which took under five months. This was no flash in the pan, for it was repeated with the F8F; but most of the 3,899 ordered in October 1944 were canceled on VJ-Day. The Bearcat's first taste of combat came a little later, fighting for the French in Indo-China.

Below: An unusual shot of an F7F-3N night fighter on trials with a 21.7 in torpedo. These 4,000 hp airplanes could also carry rockets under the wings.

Opposite upper: The chief single-seat version of the Tigercat was the F7F-3. Quite often the last three digits of the Bureau number were repeated, large, on the engine cowls (in this case from 80462).

Opposite lower: The outer wings of the Tigercat folded hydraulically; these are Dash-3 airplanes.

Grumman built 674 F8F-1s with four .50-caliber guns, 224 F8F-1B's with four 20-mm cannon, and finally 365 F8F-2s with a taller fin, including F8F-2N night fighters and -2P aircraft equipped with two guns and a recon camera. To this day the Bearcat remains one of the favorites in unlimited racing by sporting pilots, and one modified example broke a 30-year world absolute speed record for piston-engined aircraft at 482 mph.

In March 1945 Grumman's 22,100 people turned out an all-nation record of 664 military aircraft. This amazing number did not include the mockup XTB2F, planned as the successor to the TBF and carrying an amazing array of weapons at 335 mph on the power of two R-2800s – it was cancelled because there were so few Japanese ships to be sunk.

Yet, despite the frantic pressure to build wartime aircraft, Grumman was looking far ahead. The most unexpected new product line was aluminum canoes. These were smoother, much tougher and little more than half as heavy as wood/canvas canoes, and since the end of World War II the company has been the world leader in the aluminum canoe market. Grumman also built prototypes of small two/three-place light-planes, the Kitten and the amphibian Tadpole. They were good aircraft, but Grumman wisely decided not to try to compete with much cheaper existing and war-surplus machines.

Above: Last and greatest of the Gulfhawks, Gulfhawk IV was a special Bearcat with less weight and more power.
Opposite: An F8F-2 Bearcat with the U.S. Naval Reserves coming in to land at Stapleton Field in 1950.
Below: 98 lb. Joy Le Sauvage, a Grumman secretary, shows how easy it is to do portage with the new aluminum canoe.

Right: The G-72 Kitten II was one of the company's attractive light-planes. A two-seater, it had hydraulically powered landing gear and no rudders.

Below: The G-65 Tadpole was a pusher amphibian; like the Kitten it was a two-seater of spot-welded construction.

Opposite upper: The G-44A Widgeon resembled the original G-44 but had an improved planing bottom. It was built 1944-49.

Opposite lower: Though commercially a limited success, the G-73 Mallard was one of the most attractive amphibians of all time. Engines were 600-hp Wasps, and the cabin could seat up to 12.

Grumman's forte has always been powerful airplanes with a maritime connection. On April 30, 1946, the company's first postwar product ushered in a new and perhaps even more competitive era. The G-73 Mallard is generally held to be the most beautiful amphibian ever built, a perfect successor to the Goose but faster and more shapely, seating up to 12 passengers on two 600-hp Wasp engines. Alongside 76 new Widgeons for the commercial market, Grumman also produced 59 Mallards. There deserved to be more, but it was up against war-surplus DC-3s which carried twice the load (on twice the power) and could be had in almost-new condition for half the Mallard's $90,000. Thus, the Grumman amphibian tended to appeal to discerning customers, including several heads of state such as the Kings of Egypt and the Netherlands.

In the years immediately following World War II, Grumman also flew the prototypes of three totally dissimilar aircraft that were to lead to major products not only for the Navy but also, for the first time, for the newly created U.S. Air Force. The latter service was among many customers for the big Albatross utility and rescue amphibian. The other new aircraft were the XTB3F, forerunner of the Navy's AF-2 Guardian sub-killer, and the famed F9F Panther, the company's first jet. They figured prominently in the 1950s.

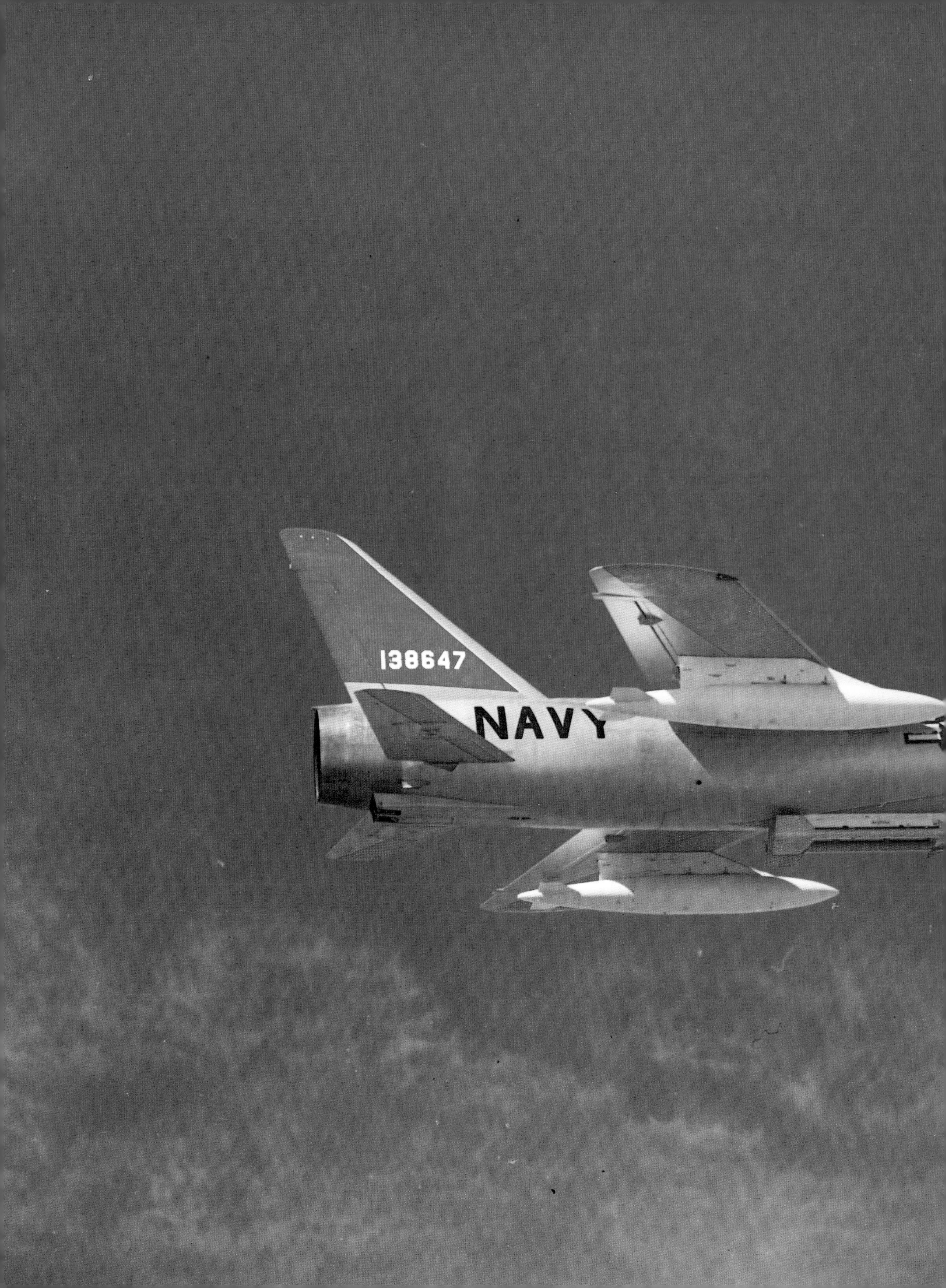
138647
NAVY

The Jet Age

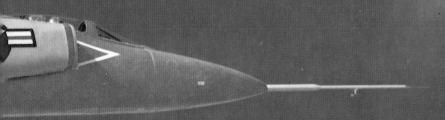

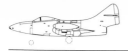

Previous page: Equipping six U.S. Navy squadrons, the F11F Tiger enjoyed considerable popularity during the late 1950s. The picture shows an F11F-1F Super Tiger carrying two external fuel tanks and a pair of AIM-9B Sidewinders.

On June 25, 1950, the army of North Korea invaded South Korea, and United Nations forces were soon drawn in to help repel the aggressor. No sane person welcomes a war, but the conflict in Korea had the immediate effect of arresting the postwar decline in U.S. airpower and in establishing wholly new levels of defense funding which have continued to this day. It certainly had a gigantic effect on Grumman, which had shrunk to a tiny fraction of its wartime peak, but which was to grow again from 1950 up to the present.

In the changed political climate of the Cold War, the Soviet Union seemed to pose the greatest threat to the free nations, and one of the biggest elements in that threat was the Soviet submarine fleet. Hundreds of wartime Avengers were modified to help deal with this menace, while Grumman worked on a successor. This new aircraft, designated the XTB3F, first flew on December 23, 1946. Fractionally bigger than the Avenger, but more streamlined, this aircraft had a 2,300-hp R-2800 on the nose and (though it was not immediately apparent) a Westinghouse turbojet in the tail. The latter was fed with air from inlets in the leading edge of each wing root, and was used only when maximum speed was needed in combat. Eventually it was decided

the booster jet was not worthwhile, and its removal made room for more crew and equipment. After further development the XTB3F became the AF-2 Guardian (AF meaning "attack", Grumman – 'G' had already been allocated to another manufacturer), the first being delivered to the Navy on October 18, 1950.

Left: The Guardian was designed to operate in "hunter/killer" pairs, an AF-2 hunter working with an AF-2S killer. These aircraft, from the Naval Reserve Unit at New York, are both AF-2S killers.

Left: Named "Fertile Myrtle" because it could carry a large protruding radome, the XTB3F-1S was the immediate forerunner of the Guardian. The rear fuselage ended in a jet nozzle, but when this picture was taken the Westinghouse booster jet had been removed.

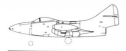

Even with just the R-2800 piston engine, the maximum speed was a healthy 317 mph (510 km/h), despite the big wingspan of 60 ft. 8 in. (18.5 m) and the loaded weight of up to 25,500 lb. (11,567 kg), a full 10,000 lb. (4,536 kg) heavier than a TBF-1. Grumman delivered the Guardian in two versions which worked together. The 153 of the AF-2W version had a crew of four and used a giant APS-20 radar and other sensors to search for submarines. The 193 of the AF-2S version had a crew of three and used a smaller APS-31 radar, sonobuoys which located submerged submarines by sound waves, and an AVQ-2 searchlight to pinpoint the target before killing it with depth charges, a torpedo or bombs. Production was completed in 1953 with 40 AF-3S Guardians carrying a new sensor, a magnetic anomaly detector (MAD). The MAD senses the small disturbance caused by a submarine to the Earth's magnetic field. To avoid interference from the aircraft's own metal parts the MAD is carried as far away as possible, on the end of a long boom projecting aft of the tail.

Opposite: The AF-2W Guardian was one of the biggest single-engined carrier-based aircraft ever built, with a span of over 60 ft. (18.3 m).

Below: The Guardian hunter/killer team comprised of an AF-2W (nearer, with giant search radar) and the AF-2S sub-killer, seen on the right. The latter had its own APS-30 attack radar in an underwing pod.

Grumman was well known for its amphibian aircraft, and it flew its biggest amphibian for the first time on October 1, 1947. Named Albatross, it was to have many designations, partly because it was operated by the Navy, Air Force, Coast Guard, Air National Guard and numerous friendly nations. Roughly the size of a DC-3, it had a deep and capacious boat-type hull with a cockpit for two pilots and a main cabin for up to 20 passengers or 12 litter casulties. It was similar to a much bigger Goose, though the fully retracting landing gear was of the tricycle type and two 1,425-hp Wright Cyclone engines gave well over three times the Goose's power. Originally designed as a utility transport and for air/sea rescue, the stately Albatross was developed to fly transport, reconnaissance, maritime patrol and even anti-submarine missions. Two prototype aircraft were identified as XJR2F-1. Production versions were designated UF-1 for the Navy and Coast Guard, and SA-16A for the Air Force. Later "B" versions of the aircraft had a larger wing span and a fixed camber – instead of leading edge slats – and a taller fin. Their designation was subsequently changed to the HU-16 series. During the Vietnam war, flying mainly from Da Nang, the HU-

16B rescued a total of 60 downed airmen – on occasions racing North Vietnamese junks to the vital life raft. Altogether Grumman built 464 Albatrosses over a period of 14 years.

In the late 1940s Grumman had taken a cool look at the helicopter, and decided - probably very wisely – to stick with fixed wings. One of the things it knew best was the carrier-based ASW mission, and when in 1951 the Navy ran a competition for an airplane able to perform both the hunter and killer mission – instead of needing two aircraft operating as a team – Grumman quickly submitted a completely new design, the G-89. Many rival companies fought for what promised to be a major program, and Grumman's submission was one of the least detailed. But from its earliest days the company had a reputation for delivering at least as much as it promised. During World War II, Vice-Admiral John S. McCain said: "The name Grumman on a plane or part has the same meaning to the Navy that 'Sterling' on silver has to you." So the simple proposal was the one that was picked, and the result was that on December 4, 1952, the first prototype XS2F-1 Tracker made its maiden flight.

Grumman achieved a breakthrough with the S2F (later S-2) Tracker in packaging everything needed by a hunter/killer team into one airplane and still making it compact enough to operate from a carrier. This S2F-1 (BuNo 136691) has its search radar and MAD boom both extended.

Main picture: Grumman scored another success with the big Albatross amphibian, finding many customers and sustaining a very long production life. It is rather heavier and more powerful than a DC-3, and even more versatile.

Inset above right: This Albatross was built for the Air Force as an SA-16A and brought up to long-span, big-tail SA-16B standard. Note the insignia of the Strategic Air Command.

Inset below right: Grumman amphibians in unique formation in the late 1940s, a G-44A Widgeon leading a Navy JRF-5 Goose and a Mallard.

Designation: S-2A TRACKER.
Type: Anti-submarine.
Powerplant: Two Wright R-1820-82WA Cyclones air-cooled radials, 1,525 hp each.
Wingspan: 69 ft 8 in; later 72 ft 7 in.
Length: 42 ft 3 in.
Height: 16 ft 3 in.
Weight: 17,357 lb; later 26,867 lb.
Maximum Speed: 287 mph at 5,000 ft.
Ceiling: 23,000 ft.
Range: 900 miles.
Armament: 4,810 of bombs.
Crew: 4.
Users: USN.

Right: The Royal Australian Navy used the Tracker for over 25 years, and when half the force was destroyed in a hangar fire in 1982 they were immediately replaced with S-2s from U.S. Navy inventory.

Like the Albatross, it had a long-span wing mounted in the high position and carried two R-1820 Cyclone engines. There resemblance stopped, because the wings folded (up and over on slightly diagonal hinges to lie beside each other above the center section), and the rather wide fuselage was packed with equipment to fly the challenging mission. At the front was a comfortable cockpit for pilot and copilot. Two crewmen sat in the rear to manage the ASW sensors. The latter included APS-38 radar in a retractable belly radome, a magnetic anomaly detector in the tip of a long tube which could be extended far behind the tail when in use, a 70-million candlepower searchlight on the right wing, and 16 sonobuoys ejected through aft-facing tubes in the rear of the engine nacelles. The center fuselage incorporated an internal weapons bay which could accommodate two torpedoes or depth bombs or a variety of other stores, while six 5-inch (127-mm) rockets or depth bombs could be carried under the wings. Black de-icer boots on the wings and tail made sure freezing rain and other icing conditions did not cause problems, and thanks to almost full-span slotted flaps, slotted outer wings and powerful flight controls, including both ailerons and spoilers for roll control, the Tracker proved able to lift heavy loads of sensors, weapons and fuel, take off from a short deck without a catapult, fly remarkably slowly under precise control, and yet react quickly in combat.

It was simply another big winner for Grumman. Again like the Albatross, it stayed in production for a long time, and for many customers, but the numbers were greater. When the last was flown out of Bethpage in December 1967 it was No. 1,167 off the line, and another 100 had been made under license by de Havilland Aircraft of Canada. They had been produced in many versions, which after 1962 were designated from S-2A to S-2G, with numerous conversions for flight training, electronics training, utility transport, target towing and photo reconnaissance.

Carriers at sea naturally need to make use of their capability as a floating airfield to fly in urgent stores, mail, visitors, or crew joining the ship, and to fly out visitors, critically sick or injured crew and such items as costly airplane parts needing special attention. This COD

Left: In 1986 Grumman St. Augustine was busy refurbishing S-2E Trackers for the Turkish Navy.

Below: Wider-bodied than a Tracker, the C-1A Trader was the world's first purpose-designed COD (carrier on-board delivery) transport.

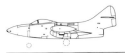

(carrier on-board delivery) mission had always been flown very inefficiently by carrier-capable warplanes such as the TBM. With the introduction of giant new carriers of the *Forrestal* class, such hand-to-mouth arrangements could be inadequate, and a proper COD transport was clearly needed. The obvious basis for such an airplane was the Tracker, and on January 28, 1955, Grumman began delivering 87 TF-1 (later redesignated C-1A) Traders. These were basically Trackers without ASW gear, but with an enlarged fuselage accommodating nine passengers in aft-facing seats or a cargo load of 3,500 lb. (1,588 kg). With full capability for catapult launches and arrested landings, the Traders brought home to the Navy what it had been missing in not having had a proper COD aircraft previously. Four were greatly modified as EC-1As, with as many as 70 antennas linked to high-powered electronics to teach crewmen the dark art of ECM (electronic countermeasures), which has become a major weapon in warfare.

Another major electronic weapon is the high-powered airborne surveillance radar. Such a radar can see much farther than it could at sea level, and with sufficient power and clarity it can keep track of every aircraft, every ship and almost every moving object within a radius of 230 miles (370 km). Thus, such a radar can provide such vital functions as AEW (airborne early warning), for example, by spotting hostile aircraft while they are still far beyond the horizon to observers at low level, or can give directions to friendly attack aircraft or to individual airplanes that are caught in bad weather or in any other kind of trouble. The very first airplane to carry an AEW radar was a Grumman Avenger in 1943, and this led to the special Avengers equipped with APS-20 radar in the early 1950s. But by this time much bigger and more powerful radars were available, such as the APS-82, and bigger aircraft

The WF-2 Tracer was the world's first purpose-designed carrier-based AEW (airborne early-warning) aircraft. Based on the C-1A Trader, it was packed with radar with the antenna rotating inside a giant fixed radome, unlike its successor, the Hawkeye. The designation gave rise to the nickname Willy Fudd, which continued even though the designation was soon changed to E-1B.

were needed to bear them aloft. Again, the obvious basis was the Tracker, and plans were hatched to build two WF-1s carrying the giant new radar with its antenna sweeping round to all points of the compass inside an oval radome above the fuselage, its rear portion extended aft to link with the central fin of a new triple tail unit.

No WF-1 was built, because it was overtaken by the WF-2, using the more capacious fuselage of the Trader. On February 28, 1958, Grumman began the delivery of 88 production WF-2 Trackers (affectionately known in the Navy as "Willy Fudds"), which joined AEW squadrons VAW-11 and VAW-12 to revolutionize the whole concept of warfare at sea. By today's standards the radar horizon was limited by many shortcomings in the APS-82 radar and by the WF-2s ceiling of 15,800 ft. (4,816 m), but in comparison with all previous history the possibilities were exciting. The obvious response of the Navy was to think, "What if we got far more powerful radar and a far more powerful airplane to carry it?" This was to provide business for Grumman in the 1960s.

In World War II the Navy had supported its long-time contractor for steam turbines, Westinghouse, in its entry into the new field of axial turbojets. The latter tended to be neat and slim in comparison with the Whittle-derived centrifugal engines, but short on thrust. Thus, when in January 1945 Grumman began to plan its G-79 design, to meet a Navy requirement for a jet night fighter, no fewer than four of the Westinghouse engines – two in each wing – had to be installed in order to obtain the specified flight performance. The engines were to be located in nacelles which were actually bulged wing sections. Though far from ideal it was the best that could be done, and on April 22, 1946, prototypes were ordered as the XF9F-1.

Designation: F9F-2 PANTHER.
Type: Fighter.
Powerplant: Pratt & Whitney J42-P-6 turbojet 5,000 lb thrust.
Wingspan: 38 ft 0 in.
Length: 37 ft 3 in.
Height: 11 ft 4 in.
Weight: 19,494 lb.
Maximum Speed: 550 mph at 22,000 ft.
Ceiling: 44,600 ft.
Range: 1,353 ft.
Armament: 4 x 20 mm cannon; 2,000 lb of bombs.
Crew: 1.
Users: USN.

Below: Seen here dumping fuel from its tip tanks, BuNo 122562 was the third production Panther, an F9F-2. These airplanes set a wholly new standard of carrier-based fighter performance and reliability.

By this time, however, Grumman was aware of the British Rolls-Royce Nene turbojet, which offered 5,000 lb. (2,268 kg) of thrust for a weight of only 1,700 lb. (771 kg), together with reliability no U.S. gas turbine could match at that time.

Grumman went to the Navy and proposed a single-seat, single-engine Nene-powered fighter as an alternative to the XF9F-1. Grumman maintained the initiative and bought two Nenes from Rolls-Royce to put into its new prototype, the XF9F-2. It was agreed that Pratt & Whitney should build the J42, an Americanized Nene, under license. The famed Connecticut company, supplier of engines for so many of Grumman's fighters, had to modify the British jet for mass-production, and to run on American fuel as well as the original fuel, kerosene, and still deliver the first J42 in October 1948, in time for production of the F9F-2. The latter, of course, needed just one of the powerful new turbojets, and the result was one of the neatest and most practical jet fighters of its day. The engine was fed via air inlets in the thickened roots of the wing and the jet nozzle was well forward under the tail. To increase lift for slow carrier landings the wings had drooping leading edges pivoted down under hydraulic power, and a mix of plain and split flaps. These were also powered hydraulically, as were the tricycle landing gear and the wing-fold jacks which raised the outer wings upwards until the streamlined auxiliary fuel tanks at their tips almost touched above the aircraft. Armament consisted of four 20-mm cannons in the nose, plus wing racks for bombs or rockets. Other features new to Grumman were an ejection seat and a pressurized cockpit.

The first of the two XF9F-2 prototypes was flown by Corwin H. "Corky" Meyer on November 21, 1947. He was not sure the speedy jet could stop on the Bethpage runway, so he made the Panther's first landing on the first incomplete runway amidst the barren expanse of Idlewild, which today is New York JFK Airport. The stopping distance was fine, and he roared off again and brought the XF9F back to its home field.

This was the start of Grumman's biggest program of the 1950s, transcending in dollar volume even the mighty F6F and TBF programs of World War II. It goes without saying that from the start the F9F was more than just satisfactory, and in the Korean war it was by far the number one Navy fighter, vastly boosting the numbers built. The initial F9F-2 version entered service with Navy squadron VF-51 in May 1949, and eventually Grumman delivered 567, as well as 54 originally delivered with the Allison J33 engine as an insurance against problems with the J42 but later converted to F9F-2 standard. The Allison engine was also to have powered the F9F-4, but these 109 airplanes were eventually converted to F9F-5s with the powerful J48, an improved J42 rated at 7,200 lb. (3,266 kg) thrust, raising maximum speed from 526 to 579 mph (932 km/h). Grumman built 616 Dash-5s, with a longer fuselage and taller vertical tail, and 36 camera-equipped F9F-5P reconnaissance aircraft. Panthers were the first Navy jets in combat. On July 3, 1950, two aircraft from VF-51 shot down a Yak-9, scoring the Navy's first jet kill, and four months later the CO of VF-111 shot down one of the swept-wing MiG-15s.

Below: The tough F9F-2 easily withstood the crash barrier arrestment.

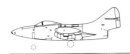

Above: A TF9F Cougar being
towed across the deck of USS
Saratoga, with an F11F Tiger
being prepared for a catapault
launch in the background.

The MIG-15's swept-back wings and tail made it faster than the
Panther, but it was not nearly as tough. No wonder the company
became affectionately known to Navy pilots as the "Grumman Iron
Works." Its airplanes, built for the incredibly tough life aboard
carriers, absorbed battle damage and came back for more. In one brief
period eight pilots of VF-52 took direct hits from 40-mm flak shells big
enough to bring down most aircraft, let alone a small fighter; all eight
pilots returned. But toughness is one thing; being too slow is another.
Grumman had already planned a swept-back version of the F9F, and
the first F9F-6 Cougar flew on September 20, 1951, hitting 650 mph
(1,046 km/h). Grumman went on to deliver 1,985 of progressively
improved Cougars, culminating in the impressive F9F-8, which despite
being much heavier could reach 690 mph (1,110 km/h). Many of this
final version were -8P photo versions and -8T dual-control trainers.
After 1962 the trainers were redesignated as TF-9J's, and four even
soldiered on into the Vietnam War, serving in combat as FAC (Forward
Air Control) aircraft, a role never envisaged when the first Panther flew
20 years earlier. Total output of F9F's was 3,370, most of which were built
at Bethpage. The F9F-6 was built at Calverton, Long Island.

The F9F began with a "straight" (unswept) wing and finished with
one swept back at 35^0. To many it seemed obvious that the ideal
solution would be an airplane whose wings were pivoted, so that they

could be spread out to a wide span for low-speed carrier takeoffs and landings, and for low-speed loitering flight, and swept back under pilot control for a dash at supersonic speed when necessary. Bell had tested the X-5 with a ground-adjustable set of wings covering a range of sweep angles, and as early as January 1948 Grumman and the Navy Bureau of Aeronautics began discussing a fighter with what today are often called "swing wings." On July 7, 1949, the company made a formal proposal, and the following year two XF10F-1 Jaguar prototypes were ordered, the first flying at Edwards Air Force Base in California on May 19, 1952. A portly oddball of an aircraft, it bristled with strange features, and ran into a host of problems, the worst being concerned with the J40 engine and with basic stability and control. The XF10F was terminated in May 1953, but the swing-wing concept had shown such promise that Grumman never regretted building the world's first variable-sweep fighter, and the experience was ultimately to lead to today's peerless F-14 Tomcat.

The company's next fighter was also destined never to be a major front-line aircraft, but the contrast with the XF10F could hardly have been greater. The Grumman G-98 design evolved into one of the neatest, smoothest and most attractive small jets ever built. It was the first production Navy fighter to exceed the speed of sound in level flight with the aid of an afterburner.

Above: One of only two XF10F-1 Jaguar prototypes ordered by the Navy Bureaux of Aeronautics, coming in to land at Edwards Air Force Base in California. This strange looking machine was the worlds first "swing-wing" aircraft and despite being a short lived project provided invaluable knowledge for Grumman aircraft to come.

The aircraft was conceived as a supersonic version of the F9F, and received the designation F9F-8. But when the same designation was given to what ultimately became the Cougar, the new fighter became the F9F-9 Tiger. It was a totally new design, and accordingly in 1955 it became the F11F-1. And under the revised 1962 designation system, it became the F-11A. Through all these paper changes, the aircraft itself remained one of the most successful and trouble-free Grumman ever built.

The most striking feature of the Tiger was its fuselage design, which was based on the new "area rule" concept developed in 1952 by Dave Whitcomb of the National Advisory Committee for Aeronautics. The area rule was a new design principle that promised to reduce wave drag in transonic and supersonic aircraft.

According to the area rule, wave drag is proportional to an aircraft's cross section area. Accordingly, an aircraft's total cross section area, and hence its drag, can be reduced by smoothly contouring or narrowing the fuselage at the wing roots.

The concave fuselage gave the Tiger a distinct "Coke bottle" profile. Ahead of the wing, the lateral inlets were thrust forward to feed air to the Wright J65 after burning turbojet located in the tail section. The wing was mounted·in the mid position, and the main cover skins were milled from single plates of aluminum (a new manufacturing method in 1953). Small wing tips were manually foldable—down for simplicity. The fully powered controls – used by Grumman for the first time on this aircraft – consisted of roll wing spoilers, a rudder and a "slab" horizontal tail with a geared elevator. The wing trailing edge out to the fold joint was a slotted high-lift flap, with companion powered slats on the leading edge. With typical Grumman cleverness, sufficient fuel was contained in the fighter's integral wing and fin tanks and fuselage cells. All three units of the landing gear retracted into the fuselage, the nose gear having twin wheels. Under the fuselage were four 20 mm cannons and provision was later made for underwing pylons to launch the Navy's new Sidewinder air-to-air missile, or limited surface-attack weapons. Altogether it was a very attractive new bird, though overall capability was inevitably limited by its modest size and engine power.

The Navy did, however, buy 199 production F11F-1 Tigers with the J65 engine. When Corky Meyer flew the first example without afterburners on July 30, 1954, he thought it the smoothest ride ever. In later flights, the F11F effortlessly slipped through the sound barrier to

The Tiger, which originally was known as the F9F-9, was one of the first aircraft ever designed to the newly discovered area rule, which describes how to reduce wave drag in supersonic or transonic flight. The visible result was what became known as a "Coke bottle" fuselage, clearly visible from below. The missiles are early Sidewinders.

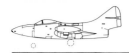

Designation: F-11A TIGER
Type: Fighter bomber.
Powerplant: Wright J65-4 turbo-jet with afterburner. 11,000 lb thrust.
Wingspan: 31 ft 7½ in.
Length: 44 ft 11 in.
Height: 13 ft 3 in.
Weight: 22,160 lb.
Maximum Speed: 890 mph.
Ceiling: 50,500 ft.
Range: 700 miles
Armament: 4 x 20 mm cannon & 4 x AIM-9C or similar. Sidewinder AAM.
Crew: 1.
Users: USN.

hit March 1. 1, or 742 mph (119km/h) at high altitude, using the J65s afterburner which boosted sea level thrust to 10,500 lb. (4,463 kg). Grumman then delivered 42 F11F-1s on a first contract. (They were equipped with a slim nose, tipped by a flight-refueling probe). These were followed by 157 on a second contract with a longer nose for a radar gunsight with the FR probe moved to the right side. The first of six Navy squadrons to re-equip with the Tiger was VA-156 in March 1957. Tigers served with considerable popularity until 1960, only yielding to the introduction of the much bigger and more powerful Chance Vought F8U (later the F8) Corsair. The Tiger was also one of the most popular mounts of the Navy's famed Blue Angels formation aerobatic team.

No account of the F11F would be complete without mentioning that one Tiger managed to shoot itself down. On September 21, 1956, test pilot Tom Attridge was engaged in testing the guns during high-speed dives over the Atlantic. Suddenly the engine flamed out and refused to start, and Attridge was lucky to make Long Island and execute a belly landing. What had happened was the supersonic fighter had overtaken some of its own 20-mm bullets as the latter slowed down. The bullets were ingested into the engine's air intake, damaging the engine compressor blades.

In 1955 Grumman and the Navy decided to modify two F11F-1 aircraft to accept and test out the new, more powerful General Electric J79 engine. The fuselage was enlarged and the inlets were redesigned to handle engine airflow in Mach 2+ flight. Wing fillets and ventral fins were also added. The aircraft was airlifted to Edwards Air Force Base where it flew for the first time on May 22, 1956. It performed superbly and became the first Navy fighter aircraft to exceed Mach 2 in level flight. It briefly held the world's altitude record of 76,940 feet in zoom climbs. Two F11F-1F's were built, but the Navy never ordered any production versions because the aircraft did not have the range or versatility of the F8U Crusader then in production.

After 1956 it was obvious to Grumman that the company was going to miss out on the development of one major generation of Navy fighters, but new designs for other duties proliferated as never before, and employment climbed from 13,000 in the middle of the decade to 14,500 at its end. Most of the new airplanes on the drawing board figure in the next chapter, but one, the Ag-Cat, was in full service in 1959 and triggered off a wholly new line of business.

As often is the case at meetings of stockholders, at a Grumman stockholders' meeting in 1956 Roy Grumman invited suggestions for diversifying the company's products. Joe Lippert, an aerodynamicist who left his mark on many Grumman airplanes, asked, "Why not build an aircraft specifically for agricultural operation?" At that time agricultural aviation, involving the supply of airplanes for spraying and dusting crops, was already big and growing much bigger. The requirements for such aircraft are almost the reverse of those for fighters. The ag-plane must be extremely tough and corrosion-proof, but it has to fly slowly rather than fast. It must retain full control in tight turns at the lowest possible height while carrying heavy loads. A particular requirement is that, should it fly into an obstruction and crash, the pilot must be able to walk away and, if possible, the airplane should be repairable.

Virtually every existing ag-plane was a former wartime trainer, such as the Boeing Kaydet biplane, or occasionally a jerry-built design based on a combat machine. They were uneconomic, often dangerous, and proliferated only because they were cheap. Grumman saw at once that the market was waiting for a new aircraft which, even if more costly, could cover greater areas of crops in less time, with less fuel and a totally new level of safety. In September 1956 design began of the G-164 Ag-Cat, a throwback to the biplane era but actually designed to incorporate the latest technology. A big single-seater, it could have almost any engine from 220 to 600 horsepower, and ahead of the lofty cockpit was a glassfiber tank for 247 U.S. gal. (206 Imp gal, or 936 litres) of liquid or 2,000 lb (907 kg) of powder chemicals. First flown on May 27, 1957, the Ag-Cat proved an immediate success, but to avoid the high overheads of a military plant, the job of churning them out in quantity was entrusted to a famed builder of gliders, Schweizer Aircraft, of Elmira, New York. By 1979 Schweizer had delivered 2,455 Ag-Cats of various models;

Above: Perhaps not a thing of beauty, but a first-rate airplane and a great commercial success, Grumman's Super Ag-Cat is a beefed-up and much more powerful machine than the original G-164 Ag-Cat. The Super was first delivered in 1966.

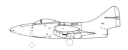

production was suspended for two years, but resumed again in 1981 as an all-Schweizer product, the licensee having purchased all rights to the design.

Ag-Cats are still being built, but another line of business in the 1950s was destined never to bring Grumman income except from research and development. This was the new field of guided missiles, and though the company's work in this field received almost zero publicity, because it was highly classified, Grumman worked on two giant programs right at the leading edge of contemporary technology and very nearly achieved major production weapons.

The first Grumman missile was the Rigel. Developed during the late 1940s, it was designed to be fired from a surfaced submarine and carry a nuclear or large conventional warhead with high precision to a target far beyond the horizon. Early test vehicles had an integral ramjet body and a tandem boost rocket motor. But the much bigger definitive TM (Tactical Missile) had canard foreplanes for control, large rear wings carrying twin ramjets on their tips, and four boost rockets arranged round the rear body to blast the mighty cruise missile out of the submarine launch tube. This weapon weighed 25,000 lb. (11,340 kg) at launch and was much longer than a Cougar or Tracker. It could carry a 3,000-lb. (1,361 kg) warhead a distance of 576 miles (927 km) at twice the speed of sound, but for reasons having little connection with the test results the project was terminated in early 1953.

The other Grumman-designed missile was the Navy's AAM-N-10 Eagle, an air-to-air weapon having a performance so much greater than any predecessor that it threatened, or promised, to revolutionize the whole of air combat. Grumman was responsible for the airframe, propulsion integration and ground equipment, in partnership with many other companies led by Bendix. At launch the giant missile was over 16 ft. (4.9m) long, and weighed 1,284 lb. (582 kg). First, it was blasted away by a solid rocket boost motor, reaching no less than Mach 4 (about 2,750 mph/4,426 km/h). The rocket then fell away to the rear, making the remaining missile shorter and lighter, so that its own internal rocket could propel it at high speed to targets up to 127 miles (204 km) away, finally homed-in by the missile's own nose-mounted radar. Not least of the radical features of Eagle was that its performance was so great that the launching fighter became almost secondary. Indeed, recognizing this, the Navy contracted with Douglas to build prototypes of the XF6D-1 Missileer, a relatively slow aircraft whose job was to take off from a carrier and lift six of the big missiles to 30,000 feet. Each missile could then pick out its own target and fly unerringly towards it, killing at unprecedented distances.

Perhaps shortsightedly, the outgoing Navy Secretary in 1960, Thomas S. Gates Jr, cancelled the aircraft and the missile; certainly the concept of a fighter unable to fly at high supersonic speeds was by 1960 difficult to comprehend. This paved the way for Grumman's participation in developing a much faster fighter, the F-111B. The Eagle led to the big Phoenix missiles which were intended to be carried by the F-111B but which actually joined the Navy carried by Grumman's own F-14A Tomcat. Few people today know that the technology of the long range AAM, able to stand off and kill from great distances, was pioneered by Grumman.

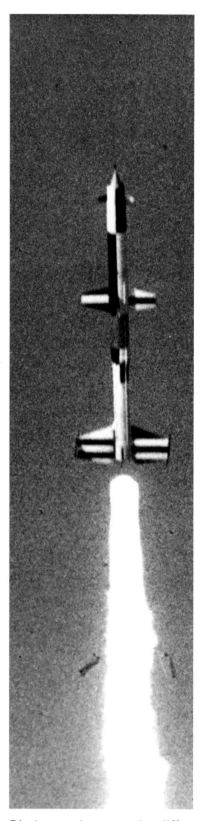

Rigel came in two quite different configurations. The launch (above) is the original model: the launcher loading test (opposite) shows the twin-engine tactical model.

To the Moon and Back

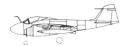

By 1960 times were changing in aerospace. Famous old names disappeared through mergers or even an inability to continue operations. It was becoming a very serious world indeed, where not thousands of dollars but millions or even billions hinged on the quality of management, on technology so new that it became difficult to describe to the layman, and on the continuing ability of a company to get everything right the first time. Major aerospace customers – famed airlines, and the armed forces – tried as far as possible to spell out their requirements in the form of detailed numerical values; but, perhaps even more than before, a company's track record was what counted.

It is doubtful whether anyone in the upper echelons of the Navy was unaware of Grumman's reputation. The solid Iron Works had been described as the nation's savior in fighting the Japanese. "Thank God for Grumman," said one wartime admiral. The management – still the original close–knit team, except for the sad loss of Jake Swirbul in 1960 – was determined to keep and even enhance that unique reputation. In 1960, prototypes of two new Navy airplanes took to the air to launch programs not only still filling the Bethpage plants but certain to do so for years to come. And further business in the 1960s came from a strange bug-eyed airplane built for a new customer: the Army.

In fact, after the Korean war both Army and Marine Corps had identified a need for a battlefield reconnaissance airplane. It was to be neither a lightplane, such as had been used for this role in the past, nor a fast jet, but somewhere in between. Powered by twin turboprop engines, it was to have high-lift devices and long-stroke landing gears to enable it repeatedly to operate from the shortest and bumpiest frontline airstrips. The OV-1's in-flight performance, maneuverability and engine power were rather like those of a World War II fighter, but it was a little bigger and quite different in arrangement. In the extreme nose sat the pilot and observer side-by-side, on the Martin-Baker ejection seats that were becoming almost standard on Grumman warplanes. Giant bulged windows gave a superb view in almost all directions, and armor and flak curtains offered protection against hostile fire. Its task was to fly low over land battles while carrying cameras, an infra-red heat sensor and, in later versions, a giant SLAR (side-looking airborne radar).

Below: Though the Mohawk's biggest job to date was providing the aerial overview needed by field commanders in Vietnam, the rebuilt OV-1D has also performed many important tasks. This example carried out atmospheric measurements around the erupting Mt. St. Helens volcano in Washington state.

Grumman called this bird the G-134, while to the Army it was the OV-1 Mohawk. The Marines dropped out, but the OV-1 was flown on April 14th, 1959, and subsequently 380 were delivered in four major versions, the production line closing in December 1970. All current Mohawks in the U.S. Army are being completely refurbished and brought up to OV-1D standard with the ability to carry any of a range of sensors, to maintain a front-line force of 100, as well as a further 26 configured for the Elint (electronic intelligence) mission, designated RV-1D. Mohawks no longer carry weapons, but during the Vietnam period they toted such diverse ordnance that one was photographed with all its tanks, bombs, rockets and missiles – and a kitchen sink!

In parallel, Grumman produced another twin-turboprop that could hardly have been more different. This was the G-159 Gulfstream (later, when there were other Gulfstreams, it became the Gulfstream I). From early days Grumman had built small amphibians for the corporate and executive market, some even selling to heads of state, but the lack of big orders after the Korean war prompted a search for new products for new markets. It so happened that there already existed a group of engineers led by company pilot-salesman Henry Schiebel who had been studying the prospects for a totally new transport to meet the needs of big corporate customers and possibly even a few airlines. The trouble was, whatever its attractions, it was likely to cost around $1 million, compared with $200,000 for a good DC-3.

Above: Following tests in 1964 with special JOV-1C Mohawks flown by the 11th Air Assault Division, many OV-1s carried weapons in Vietnam. This example is firing rockets from outboard underwing pods. Color at that time was olive drab, today changed to grey.

Designation: OV-1D MOHAWK.
Type: Battlefield reconnaissance.
Powerplant: Two AVCO Lycoming T53-L-701 turboprops, 1,400 eshp each.
Wingspan: 48 ft 0 in.
Length: 41 ft 0 in.
Height: 13 ft.
Weight: 11,800 lb.
Maximum Speed: 251 mph.
Ceiling: 25,000 ft.
Range: 820 miles.
Armament: Usually none.
Crew: 2.
Users: U.S. ARMY.

Inset: U.S. Army No. 62-5903 was built as an 0V-1B, the first version of the Mohawk to carry the SLAR (side-looking airborne radar) and also introducing many other changes including an increased wingspan. The triple-finned tail was needed for single-engine stability and for control at the very low airspeeds at which the OV-1 could fly. Black strips on leading edges are de-icers.

Main Picture: No. 67-18898 was one of three OV-ID pre-production aircraft which were used to develop today's definitive OV-ID multirole aircraft able to carry cameras, infra-red or (as seen here) a SLAR.

UNITED STATES ARMY

718898

After prolonged study and discussion it was decided to go ahead with a low-wing machine smaller than the DC-3 but considerably faster, able to use almost any civil field and climb up to cruise in pressurized comfort at 355 mph (571 km/h) at 30,000 feet. Compared with the first executive jet, the Lockheed JetStar, it would be more capacious, seating up to 24 passengers, and fly very much farther on any given fuel burn. But would it sell? A rival said Grumman would sell "from 15 to 17" and lose its shirt.

The engine picked was the Rolls-Royce Dart Mk 529, rated at 2,180 equivalent horsepower and with proven reliability. Another thing in the Gulfstream's favor was looks; it looked as smooth as it flew. The prototype flew on August 14, 1958, and it was soon obvious that the many potential customers who had urged Schiebel on were prepared to back their opinion with money. Sales soon went beyond "15 to 17," most being luxurious company airplanes configured for 10 to 12 seats. Even the Navy bought nine TC-4C trainers with bulbous radomes to train pilots and bombardier/navigators to fly Grumman's own A-6 Intruder. Altogether 200 Gulfstream Is were sold and have flown with essentially perfect reliability to this day and will continue service well into the next century. Some have been stretched into Gulfstream 1-C Commuters, seating 37 passengers for normal local-service airline operation.

Such aircraft were instrumental in broadening the company's product base, but its staple income continued to come from the Navy. The next important program for that customer was to be one of the biggest and most enduring of the company's entire history, the basic design being completed in 1959 and the latest upgraded production version not even being due for delivery until 1990. This airplane is, of course, the A-6 Intruder.

During the Korean war, the most commmon type of mission was the

Below: With its twin Rolls Royce Dart 529 turbo-props, the G-159 Gulfstream I opened up the executive aircraft market. Its elegant lines and advanced avionics gave Grumman a world beater.

attack on a surface target. Commanders had a choice of fast jets, which might get back unscathed but which burned a lot of fuel, carried very few bombs or rockets and could not fly at all in bad weather. Even in good conditions, weapon delivery accuracy depended entirely on pilot skill and was, to put it kindly, highly variable. The alternative was a tough propeller airplane, such as a Skyraider; this could tote a lot of bombs and rockets but it was very vulnerable, exhausted its pilots in ten-hour round trips and still had problems in accurate delivery and in bad weather. The solution was self-evident: a really capable fast jet with a big weapon load and plenty of avionics for accurate delivery of ordnance no matter what the weather.

In 1957 eight companies submitted 11 designs to try to win what had every indication of becoming a major Navy program. On the last day of that year the Grumman G-128 submission was chosen, and the first A2F-1 (later redesignated A-6A) Intruder made its maiden flight on April 19, 1960. Perhaps the most remarkable aspect of the A-6A was that it appeared so deceptively unremarkable. But looks can be deceiving. Inside the A-6A was the world's most advanced integrated computer controlled attack system. On the exterior, for short takeoff and landing performance, the jetpipes from the two 9,300lb. thrust Pratt & Whitney J52-8A turbojets were hinged, so that at takeoff they could be angled downwards to help provide lift. This rather ineffectual idea was soon discarded, leaving two ordinary engines tucked closely into the sides of the fuselage under the mid-mounted wings. The latter relied upon a long span for good low-speed lift, backed up by full-span leading-edge and trailing-edge flaps to give sharp camber at low speeds. Speed brakes on the fuselage were later supplemented by unusual looking wingtip speed brakes that split open to slow the aircraft. Roll control was provided by long flaperons on the upper surface ahead of the flaps, which served as ailerons and also as lift spoilers. The fuselage

Below: One of the design features of the A-6 is its speed brakes which comprise the split trailing edge of each wingtip, opening above and below. They can be seen on every landing approach, such as this carrier landing by an A-6E in the 1980s.

Below: The A-6 Intruder has already served the Navy and Marines for almost 25 years and bore a tremendous burden of night and bad-weather attack missions over North Vietnam. These A-6A's were pictured while flying with Navy attack squadron VA-176 "Thunderbolts," home based at NAS Oceana, Virginia, but embarked at sea aboard the carrier USS *Franklin D. Roosevelt*.

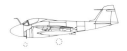

Main picture: A-6As of Marine All Weather Attack Squadron 224 *"Bengals"* operating from Cherry Point, North Carolina, in 1967. Each is carrying two 300-U.S. gallon drop tanks.

Inset: A-6As on a combat mission over North Vietnam in July 1969. The nearer aircraft has Mk 82 bombs and its companion Snakeye delayed bombs. They were flying from USS *Constellation* with VA-196 *"Main Battery."*

began with a bluff radome housing two separate radars, with a flight-refuelling probe mounted above the nose. The cockpit was arranged with side-by-side Martin-Baker seats for the pilot and bombardier/navigator. The air inlets extended past the cockpit on each side, the outer skins of the ducts incorporating a folding ladder for the crew. Aft of the cockpit the fuselage tapered away sharply to a slim profile carrying the conventional tail with a powered "slab" horizontal stabilizer. The steerable twin-wheel nose gear was stressed for nose-tow catapult shots, the 80-ton pull being enough to fling the loaded A-6 off the bow at over 150 mph. The main gear was pivoted at the rear of the wing box and retracted forward and inward to a shallow bay in the angle between the air inlet duct and the wing root. The large fuel capacity in integral wing tanks and self-sealing fuselage cells gave the Intruder a combat radius of up to 1,000 miles. It was built to carry a complete inventory of air-to-ground weapons, including missiles.

Above: By the late 1980s the A-6E's were painted in an overall gray for low visibility, with low-contrast markings. Here a TRAM-equipped A-6E unfolds its wings before being catapulted from a carrier of the 6th Fleet in the Mediterranean.

Left: Most of the aircraft seen parked aboard the *John F. Kennedy* are TRAM-equipped A-6E Intruders, but No. 606 is a four-seat EA-6B Prowler electronic counter-measures aircraft.

Opposite: Cat shot of a TRAM-equipped A-6E. Over the next few years these aircraft will be put through a major update program.

Right: Grumman A-6 airplanes aboard CV-67 *John F. Kennedy.* Nearest is an EA-6B Prowler; beyond are two TRAM A-6E Intruders and a KA-6D tanker. All these types will go on serving to the end of the century.

Far right: The cockpit of an A-6A Intruder, showing the pilot's station nearer the camera with the bombardier/navigator seated slightly farther back and lower down on the right side. Though it can be seen that the pilot had his own radar display, most of the job of operating DIANE (as mentioned on this page) and the other electronics systems was the responsibility of the right-seater.

Designation: A-6E TRAM INTRUDER.
Type: Carrier-based attack.
Powerplant: Two Pratt & Whitney J52-P-8B turbojets 9,300 lb. thrust each.
Wingspan: 53 ft. 0 in.
Length: 54 ft. 9 in.
Height: 16 ft. 2 in.
Weight: 60,626 lb.
Maximum Speed: 644 mph at sea level.
Ceiling: 42,400 ft.
Range: 1,920 miles.
Armament: 15,000 lb. of bombs.
Crew: 2.
Users: USN, USMC.

The first production A-6A's were delivered to Navy squadron VA-42 in February 1963, just in time for almost all of the massive production run of 482 of this version to see prolonged combat duty in the Vietnam war, with both the Navy and the Marine Corps. It was the first truly all-weather attack plane developed. In total darkness, rain or fog, the two-man crew could locate, identify and attack a target then land aboard an aircraft carrier – while never glancing out of the cockpit. The DIANE (Digital Integrated Attack Navigation Equipment), consisting of the radars, computers, displays and, later, such add-ons as CAINS (Carrier Aircraft Inertial Navigation System) made the A-6A a real challenge to the crews responsible for line maintenance, especially in the harsh front-line environment. Swiftly the mighty Intruder matured; 62 were converted into KA-6D tankers, each able to transfer over 21,000 lb. of fuel, and on November 10, 1970, the first A-6E took to the air. The standard model in service today is the A-6E with TRAM (Target Recognition and Attack Multisensor) in a chin turret. It has a single and much newer and more versatile radar and a totally new, more powerful computer, as well as other updates. Current A-6E's can launch the Harpoon cruise missile as a change from dropping bombloads of up to 15,000 lb. (6804 kg), which is more than a B-17 in World War II. But during the late 1980s Grumman plans to complete development of the A-6F ready for delivery from 1990. Powered by two of the new GE F404 turbojets, much smaller and burning much less fuel than the J52, yet rated at 10,800 lb. thrust, the A-6F has an almost total avionic refit from stem to stern besides adding pylons for self-defense missiles. Many of the updated avionics will be similar to those in production for a parallel Grumman upgrade program, the F-14D Tomcat. Derived aircraft, the KA-6D, EA-6A and EA-6B, are discussed in the next chapter.

The other new airplane flown in 1960 was the G-123, known to the Navy initially as the W2F-1 and very soon redesignated the E-2A Hawkeye. To the casual observer, especially one unaware of the contrast in sound, the Hawkeye appeared to be a new version of the E-1B Tracer. In fact, it was not only much bigger and more than three times as powerful but it was also the very first aircraft in history designed from a clean sheet of paper to fly the AEW (airborne early warning) mission. Indeed, so effective has the Hawkeye proved, in progressively improved versions, that it has been purchased by several land-based air forces. Thus, the penalties involved in making this big airplane fold up to fit into an aircraft carrier must have been minimal, and it remains an outstanding example of aeronautical engineering.

Above: The three Mission Specialists at work in the ATDS compartment of an E-2C Hawkeye. To the uninitiated this compartment looks much the same in all Hawkeyes, but in fact the entire radar and processing system has been repeatedly upgraded. Today the Hawkeye is a mature AEW aircraft which has been bought by several land-based air forces.

Compared with the Tracer, the Hawkeye is obviously bigger, and in the latest version the twin Allison T56 turboprops put out 5,250 horsepower each, turning propellers with four extremely broad paddle-type blades. The long outer wings fold in a traditional sto-wing style, using skewed hinges and a hydraulic jack to swing each panel down and around to lie beside the rear fuselage, upper surface outward, just like the wartime F4F and F6F. Prominent black rubber de-icer boots can be seen along the leading edges, including the unusual four-fin tail which is the only way to keep the overall height within the severe limitations of carrier hangars. Internally the Hawkeye has two pilots occupying the forward cockpit, and three mission specialists – the combat information center officer, air-control officer and radar operator – managing the AEW equipment far aft in the Airborne Tactical Data System compartment behind the wing. Separating the two groups of crew are the numerous avionics and computer boxes and racks accommodating the tremendously powerful General Electric radar, which in the E-2A was the APS-96. This system detected targets, out to a radius of 250 miles (370 km), via a saucer radome mounted on a pylon above the fuselage. In the Tracer the antenna had revolved inside a giant fixed radome, but in the Hawkeye there is no radome as such at all. Instead the antennas for the main radar and for the associated IFF (identification friend or foe) subsystem are all built into a circular rotodome of 24 feet (7.32 m) diameter, which rotates once every ten seconds. Its streamlined circular shape, resembling a discus, means that it has minimal effect on the aircraft's flying qualities.

Left: E-2C Hawkeyes of Navy Airborne Early Warning Squadron VAW-125 forming part of Carrier Air Wing CVW-1 aboard USS *John F. Kennedy*.

Below left: This Hawkeye is operational with the Japanese Air Self Defense Force.

Below: An early E-2B Hawkeye on carrier takeoff, the broad propeller blades wringing spirals of visible vapor from the moist atmosphere.

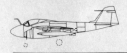

The first E-2A flew on October 21, 1960, and service with squadron VAW-11 began in January 1964. Grumman delivered 56 of this version, all later upgraded to E-2B standard with a new computer and other improvements. This was still an interim model, and the definitive basic variant, the E-2C, first flew on January 20, 1971, initially with the APS-120 radar and later with the APS-125. These impressive radars have performance of a totally different order from the original APS-96, especially when operating over land, where background clutter becomes much more of a problem. The APS-125 introduced an Advanced Radar Processing System for automatically locating and tracking targets under all combat conditions. Externally, E-2C aircraft equipped with the powerful new radars could be identified by the giant ducted radiator above the fuselage ahead of the wing to remove excess heat from the avionics vapor-cycle cooling system. In 1983 the radar was upgraded yet again, to the APS-138, all previous E-2C's being progressively upgraded. The 138s TRAC-A (total radiation aperture

control antenna) reduces unwanted sidelobes and does much more to counter advanced hostile jamming. This remarkable radar, current in E-2C production, can detect and track a small cruise missile seen end-on at over 100 miles, and can simultaneously track more than 600 targets and control more than 20 interceptions by friendly fighters. Not least, the E-2C also carries receiver antennas in the nose and tail and on the sides of the outer vertical tail fins. This equipment via the passive detection system, can detect, locate, identify and warn of enemy radars, radios and other emitters out to twice the distance that can be covered by the aircraft's own radar.

Small wonder that, while Grumman will go on building E-2C's for the Navy at six per year well into the 1990s, others have been sold to Israel, Japan, Egypt and Singapore. Many updates are planned for the future, including an even more powerful APS-145 radar system.

Just as the E-1 Tracer formed an excellent basis for the C-1 Trader COD aircraft, so has the E-2 proved to be an almost ideal basis for the Navy's current COD transport, the C-2A Greyhound. As is the case with the AEW aircraft, this new-generation transport is many times more capable than its predecessors. As an exercise in packaging it has few rivals, because although it is a substantial passenger and cargo aircraft with a rear ramp door able to admit large crates, pallets and vehicles, it still folds into a compact shape to fit into a carrier hangar, and at the same time is stressed for the brutal shipboard routine of catapult launches and arrested landings. Compared with the Hawkeye the C-2A has an appreciably wider and deeper fuselage configured for transport, with a full-section rear ramp door and fully pressurized interior. Normal loads can include 28 passengers in aft-facing airline seats, or 39 troops, or 12 litter casualties and attendants or up to 10,000 lb (4,536 kg) of cargo, a figure raised to 15,000 lb for missions not involving carrier landings and takeoffs. Its range with the carrier payload is 1,200 miles (1,930 km). The first Greyhound flew on November 18, 1964, and is an ongoing program with cost-saving multi-year procurement of a further 39 aircraft to be delivered between 1985-89. The original order was for 19, making a total for Grumman of 58 C-2s.

Above: The C-2A Greyhound will remain at least into the next century as the Navy's COD (carrier on-board delivery) transport, providing the lifeline between shore stations and the carrier battle groups at sea.

Left: One of the first E-2C Hawkeyes was this airplane assigned to VAW-126 as part of CVW-9 embarked aboard USS *Constellation*. The large scoop above the fuselage just ahead of the wing houses the vapor-cycle cooling radiator for the avionic systems.

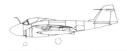

At the start of the 1960s, the U.S. Air Force had carried out prolonged studies of a TFX (Tactical Fighter Experimental) to replace most of the existing fighter and attack aircraft in the Tactical Air Command. By the end of 1960 the new Kennedy administration, and especially Secretary of Defense Robert S. McNamara, could see strong parallels between the TFX specifications and the Navy's requirement for a Fleet Air Defense fighter. It appeared an obvious way to effect a massive economy in defense funding to direct the Air Force and Navy to buy different versions of the same basic airplane. One of the bidders on December 6, 1961, was General Dynamics, Fort Worth, teamed in partnership with Grumman. The latter company was needed for its naval expertise. As well as handling the aft fuselage and landing gear of all versions, Grumman was to be wholly responsible for the Navy carrier-based fighter version, the F-111B. Amidst loud and prolonged arguments, the GD/Grumman team was chosen, but the F-111, despite its many brilliant features, was to have a troubled development.

Grumman's chief partners on the F-111B were Hughes Aircraft for the AWG-9 radar fire-control system and new AIM-54A Phoenix long-range missiles, and Pratt & Whitney for the TF30-P-12 afterburning turbofan engines. Like the Air Force F-111A, the B model seated pilot and weapon system operator side-by-side, had long-span variable-sweep wings with excellent high-lift devices, and boasted an exceptional internal fuel capacity. Very unfortunately, the problems which followed the attempt to achieve the elusive commonality between Air Force and Navy versions were to become so severe as to cripple the entire program. The Air Force versions never did serve as fighters and, despite the development of successive versions, never did meet the

From the outset the F-111B swing-wing carrier-based fighter was handicapped by too many severe compromises, not least of which was that it was a version of a land-based airplane to meet totally different requirements of the Air Force. Throughout its troubled development, Grumman engineers knew they could create a far better Navy fighter. And they would get the opportunity to do so.

original TFX requirement. Worse, the Navy F-111B, focus of such high hopes when the first was rolled out at a ceremony at the Peconic River plant on May 11, 1965, proved to be overweight and lacking in performance. Despite prolonged efforts, Congress eventually refused funds in 1968 and on July 10 of that year the Department of Defense issued a stop-work order.

It was the first time such a thing had happened to Grumman, and in fact there was not much the company could have done about it. It had hardly any say in the original design of the F-111, and it was especially galling that most of the penalties due to inter-service commonality were off-loaded on to the Navy airplane. From early in the F-111B involvement it had been evident to Grumman that the airplane was too big, the internal fuel requirement was one of several factors making it too heavy, and the short inlets and temperamental new engines merely added to a host of technical problems that never even came near to a complete solution. Long before the F-111B was terminated in mid-1968, Grumman had a team designing a totally different and vastly better fighter. Not only would it fully meet all the Navy's requirements – uncompromised by misguided aspirations to commonality – but would set such a dramatically new standard in long-range interception and stand-off kill capacity that it would, with luck, remain the Navy fleet's mainstay well into the 21st century. Of course, other companies were looking towards the same objective, but with the Navy, Grumman's tremendous reputation (not damaged by the F-111B failure) gave the Long Island company a massive head start, to which was added the unequalled experience gained with the F-111B itself. This experience was doubly relevant in that it was logical to build the new fighter around the twin TF30 engines, AWG-9 radar and AIM-54A Phoenix missile as developed for the F-111B.

All that had to be done was jack up these items and run a new airplane underneath to tie them all together. This new airplane was, of course, the fabulous F-14 Tomcat, as described in the next chapter.

Grumman's enduring efforts to diversify and build more products for more customers had, over the years, been rewarded with more success than is usual for such attempts. Airplane builders traditionally have very high overheads, build to fantastically high standards requiring costly methods, and might turn out a good consumer item but at a prohibitively high price. Even if the price could be competitive, the contribution made to the overall balance sheet would, most likely, look like peanuts. Despite these truisms, Grumman built up product lines in fiberglass and aluminum boats, truck bodies and, in the 1960s, big and powerful hydrofoils. A hydrofoil is a boat that, as it accelerates up to high speed, progressively rises on the lift of what can only be described as wings running through the sea. At full speed the hull is lifted completely above the water, eliminating the massive drag of a submerged hull and making possible the attainment of much higher speeds. Grumman's first large hydrofoil, the *H.S. Denison*, built for the U.S. Maritime Commission, was a rakish vessel 129 feet long and lifted by three sets of surface piercing foils arranged rather like the landing gear of an airplane. At full speed its 14,000-hp General Electric gas turbine, driving a water propeller, could thrust *Denison* along at 60 knots, or 69 mph.

The scene that never was to be: artwork showing the GD/Grumman F-111B in operational service from the carrier *Enterprise*, with the pivoted wings in the various settings for takeoff, low-speed loiter, supersonic dash (airplane 109), landing and parked on deck (ahead of the island). Grumman's engineering effort on this airplane was enormous, much of it devoted to trying to shed weight and meet impossible requirements.

Grumman then switched to the use of fully submerged foils which could be retracted for harbor use and while docking, rather like the wheels of the old amphibians. First came an 80-passenger commercial ferry, *Dolphin*, operated in the Canary Islands and West Indies. Then came USS *Flagstaff*, a speedy patrol gunboat for the U.S. Navy, followed in the early 1980s by two gun/missile hydrofoils of about 100 tons built for the Israeli Navy. Grumman also played a central role in Prof. Jacques Piccard's mesoscaphe (deep-diving research sub) *Ben Franklin*, which drifted deep down inside the Gulf Stream from Palm Beach to Nova Scotia in 1969. But, while this was going on, the world's headlines were reporting perhaps the greatest human achievement to date, summed up in the famous words, "That's one small step for man..." Astronaut Neil Armstrong had stepped on to the moon's surface from the LM (Lunar Module) built by Grumman.

Right: To create the LM (Lunar Module), known earlier as the LEM (Lunar Excursion Module), Grumman had to use a tremendous amount of skilled hand work in the special clean room at Bethpage. Here an ascent stage is being mated with the desent stage below, both of them covered in thin gold foil.

Far right: First man on the moon, on July 20, 1969, was Neil A. Armstrong. He got his hand camera and took this photograph of the second man on the moon, Buzz Aldrin, as he climbed down the ladder from Lunar Module 5, named *Eagle* by the astronauts.

Opposite: The first product to be assembled in the new spacecraft Clean Room at Bethpage was the OAO, the Orbiting Astronomical Observatory. Here three of the four OAOs are seen in final assembly and checkout. Four of the 4,895-lb. (2,220 kg) spacecraft were launched at two-year intervals from 1966 to 1972.

Below: Apollo missions 12, 14, 15, 16 and 17 carried ALSEP (Apollo lunar scientific experiments package) instrumentation stations to bring back as much information as possible about the moon. In the background can be seen the Grumman Lunar Module. On the first manned mission to the moon the LM weighed 33,205 lb. (15,060 kg) later examples weighed up to 36,244 lb. (16,440 kg).

In fact, in 1960, Grumman began work on producing a series of OAOs – Orbiting Astronomical Observatories – for the U.S. National Aeronautics and Space Administration. These two-ton packages of advanced scientific instrumentation played a large part in qualifying Grumman to bid on the Lunar Module (LM) contract. Following a massive company-funded study and competition in the early 1960's, Grumman's proposal convinced NASA that the company understood and could solve the problems associated with the Lunar Module and a lunar landing. On November 7, 1962, Grumman was selected as NASA's prime contractor for the vital LM. The LM would detach itself from the Apollo Command Module orbiting round the moon and carry two astronauts safely and softly down to a specific location on the lunar surface. After the initial exploration of the moon, the astronauts, plus rock samples, would reboard the LM and, after detaching the ascent portion from the base, would fire the ascent engine in order to return to the exact lunar orbit as the Command Module, with which the Ascent Module would redock, transferring the two lunar explorers and samples to the CM for return to Earth.

This book is primarily concerned with Grumman airplanes, but there can be few people whose pulses do not race a little quicker as they think of the first trip by the Grumman LM down to the surface of the moon on July 20, 1969. Neil Armstrong, accompanied by Ed "Buzz" Aldrin, had a flawless ride down and a flawless ride back, and so did five more astronaut crews, the last visiting the moon by Grumman's transport system on December 11, 1972.

The U.S. Navy's gigantic carriers give global airpower a totally new dimension. Each is a floating city, carrying some 5,000-6,000 people to perform thousands of complex tasks. Their whole purpose is to put aircraft into the sky, and in this head-on view of CV-67 USS *John F. Kennedy* almost all the aircraft are made by Grumman. In the foreground (center and left) are the Medium Attack squadrons with the A-6E. Also present are KA-6D tankers and EA-6B Prowlers. On the right is a fighter lineup of F-14A Tomcats. In the background are the E-2C Hawkeyes and more Tomcats.

Carrier Power

The 1970's opened with Grumman's engineering team under program director Mike Pelehach working round the clock on its greatest-ever aircraft contract. The product, of course, is the F-14 Tomcat. Not least of the remarkable things about it is that the original F-14A was planned as a mere stop-gap, pending arrival of the advanced F-14B. Instead it was still in production in 1987.

In spring 1968 the Navy was faced with many options in replacing the F-111B. By the summer it had decided to request proposals for VFX-1, a multirole fighter using the same engines, radar and missiles as the F-111B, for service from 1972. It would be followed by a VFX-2 to have new engines of a type being funded jointly with the Air Force (the latter needed the engines for its FX, later the F-15). Bids came from Grumman, McDonnell Douglas, General Dynamics, Rockwell and LTV teamed with Lockheed. In December the first two were named as finalists, and on January 14, 1969, New York Senators Goodell and Javits broke the news that Grumman had won what was "expected to be the largest defense contract in history," which they estimated at $5 billion.

Awards of this magnitude are not won easily. Grumman began studying the design of the F-14 in 1966. Under the company title Design No. 303 it worked its way through over 9,000 hours of tests on models in wind tunnels. More than 2,000 aerodynamic configurations were tested, as well as nearly 400 combinations of engine air inlets and jet nozzles. By January 1968 the baseline design was the 303-60, with podded engines (carried inside straight-through ducts which virtually became the rear fuselage) and a high-mounted variable-sweep swing wing. The latter unquestionably gave the best all-round performance for a carrier-based multirole aircraft, though fixed-wing designs were studied at length. Another feature settled early on was that there must be a crew of two, the second man originally being called the Missile Control Officer but later restyled the Naval Flight Officer, and that they should be seated in tandem. This reduced drag and enabled standard Martin-Baker Mk 7A ejection seats to be used.

Below: At one of the Bethpage meetings that brought the F-14 into being were (from left) Emerson Fawkes, Grumman F-14 fleet readiness manager, Vice-Admiral Thomas F. Connolly, USN Deputy Chief of Naval Operations, (Air), Mike Pelehach, Grumman vice-president and F-14 program director, and Larry Mead, Grumman vice-president and F-14 product manufacturing director.

Eight major variations of Design 303 were studied before homing in on the winning 303E design. This was broadly the 303-60 progressively updated and refined, and with twin vertical tails. The latter had sufficient fin area within the minimum overall aircraft height and length to provide directional stability at high Mach numbers. (The twin tails also remained effective at angles of attack approaching 90 degrees. This capability, never before even approached under control in any aircraft, was discovered when the final design was in flight test.) There were many important refinements in the final design, including incorporation of an iris nozzle, with convergent and divergent inner profile; jetpipes moved closer together and forward fuselage increased in depth, giving reduced drag and better single-engine handling; a reflexed upward curve of the trailing edge between the nozzles, reducing supersonic trim drag and pitching moment; increase in wing chord to increase area from 505 to 565 sq. ft. while reducing aspect ratio from 8.15 to 7.28, to reduce weight, improve combat maneuverability and allow use of simple slotted flaps; addition of a Mach sweep programmer, which automatically swings the wings in combat for maximum agility without the need for any action by the pilot; use of differential horizontal stabilizers (tailplanes) for roll control, backed up by wing spoilers which can also be used for direct lift control for near-perfect carrier landings; addition of automatic swing-out "glove vanes" from

Above: Dozens of major configurations and thousands of detail changes were examined in arriving at the final design which was a refinement of a broad configuration called 303E. A few of the projects were made in the form of simple configuration models. Among them these two single-seaters, one of which has a fixed wing. The variable-sweep model, in many ways similar to the aircraft actually built, has its glove vanes extended.

the sharply swept leading edges of the fixed inboard portions of wing, to give further reduced supersonic trim drag and enhanced maneuverability; and a slight curvature of the wings in head-on aspect, with dihedral inboard and anhedral outboard, to enable the wings to tuck perfectly inside the upper rear fuselage at the maximum angle of 68^0. A neat detail was that the wings were designed to be moved to an "oversweep" setting of 75^0 on the ground to reduce the spotting factor (the amount of space occupied by each aircraft aboard a carrier).

Behind this very abbreviated listing lay hundreds of thousands of manhours of engineering and test time. In fact, the final design of the F-14 was one of the best in the entire history of fighter design, and for many reasons the aircraft can fairly be regarded as a classic landmark – with many features reminiscent of it to be seen in the latest Soviet fighters, such as the MiG-29 and Su-27, dating from almost a decade later. But in creating the F-14, Grumman had to have tremendous faith in its own capability. Company President Lew (Llewellyn J.) Evans considered the original contract "probably the toughest ever written by the Department of Defense." Its clauses included the following financial penalties: $440,000 for each 100 pounds overweight; $440,000 for every extra second (over the required figure) for accelerating from subsonic to high supersonic speed; $1 million for each 10 nautical miles short on escort mission radius; $1,056,000 for every knot of excess speed on carrier landing; $450,000 for each extra manhour of maintenance time needed per flight hour; and $5,000 for every day late on delivery!

Below: Everything pristine and perfect for a Navy mock-up review inspection — except for the fact that the design had still not quite reached its final perfection. At this stage of Design 303E had a single vertical tail, horizontal stabilizers (tailplanes), folding ventral fins and an armament capability including Sparrow and Phoenix missiles.

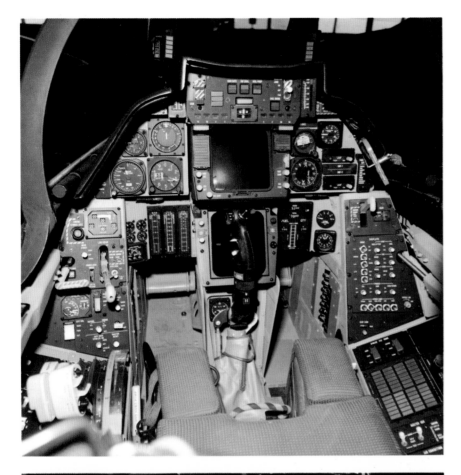

Left: The pilot's (front) cockpit of an F-14A,, which has remained without significant change right up to the emergence of the F-14A (Plus) in 1987. It is dominated by two giant electronic displays, the vertical display indicator and the horizontal situation display below it; at the top is the air combat maneuvering panel, a new idea at the time.

Left: The (rear) cockpit for the RIO (radar intercept officer) appears at first glance to resemble that for the pilot. The giant central display, however, is the tactical information display, with the detail data display panel above it; and the control stick does not fly the airplane but controls the AWG-9 radar and display.

Right: The structural heart of the F-14 is the wing center section made of titanium, which saved about 1,100 lb. (500 kg) over a steel structure. At quite a late stage this was modified so that, instead of being horizontal, it tilted up in a shallow V from the centerline, placing the outer-wing pivots higher. Under the wing carry-through box is attached a section of fuselage, consisting mainly of two engine ducts.

Below: The F-14 in an advanced stage of final assembly shows the flap and spoiler arrangement on the wings and extended speed brake between the vertical fins.

Left: A partial wing pivot structure used for structural tests.

Left: When it was designed the F-14 was very unusual in that the fuselage maintained its width right to the tail but tapered in depth until it became a mere "pancake," or beaver tail. The widely spaced TF30 engines were arranged for straight down removal, being run in and out on complex lifting dollies.

Below: The first F-14 aircraft undergoing structural testing before first flight, to verify the structural vibration modes.

Designation: F-14A TOMCAT.
Type: Carrier-based interceptor.
Powerplant: Two Pratt & Whitney TF30-P-414A turbofans, 20,900 lb. thrust each.
Wingspan: 64 ft. $1\frac{1}{2}$ in (unswept), 38 ft. 21/2 in. (swept).
Length: 62 ft. 8 in.
Height: 16 ft. 0 in.
Weight: 74,349 lb.
Maximum Speed: 1,564 mph at altitude.
Ceiling: Over 50,000 ft.
Range: 2,000 miles with external fuel.
Armament: 1 × General Electric M61A-1 20 mm multibarrel Vulcan cannon: 4 × AIM-54 Phoenix AAMs + 4 × AIM-9 Sidewinder AAMs or 14,500 lb of attack weapons.
Crew: 2.
Users: USN.

Target date for first flight of the first of 12 R & D (research and development) prototypes was January 1971. In fact, despite all sorts of problems of the kind which hit any product of such complexity, Grumman got the first bird, BuAer No. 157980, into the air ahead of time, on December 21, 1970. It was a new shape in the sky, ushering in the whole of today's era of big twin-finned highly agile fighters. Test pilots Robert Smyth and William Miller just managed a ten-minute sortie as darkness fell over the Calverton field. Flight tests began again on December 30. Suddenly, well away from its base, smoke appeared to come from the F-14. It was actually leaking hydraulic fluid; an extraordinary succession of coincidences had led to severe resonance in both of the main hydraulic systems. Control was finally lost only seconds before touchdown on the Calverton runway, but the Martin-Baker seats saved the two pilots, who just missed landing in the Tomcat's fireball. The cause was identified and eliminated, and never bothered any of the hundreds of F-14s that have followed.

There were, however, to be two other problems which were less visible but much more serious in their effects. One concerned the engines. From the outset Grumman had to design the F-14 so that, with no major airframe changes, the original TF30 engines could be replaced by the expected new-technology engines, turning the aircraft from an F-14A into an F-14B. On February 27, 1970, the Advanced Techno-

logy Engine contract was awarded to Pratt & Whitney, and on September 30, 1970, Grumman signed the contract for the F-14B, to be powered by two F401 engines, each rated at a healthy 28,090 pounds of thrust in full afterburner. The F401 first ran in September 1972, and the No. 7 R & D prototype (BuAer No. 157986) flew with two of the developmental F401s on September 12, 1973. The performance improvement was dramatic. A new engine was just what the otherwise splendid F-14A needed because, for almost 15 years, the TF30's fickel nature would mar the aircraft's magnificent record. This was finally cured by switching to a different and much more powerful engine, as related later.

After the initial engine tests in 1973, further progress on the F-14B was effectively stalled by the second major problem with the program. That problem threatened the company's very existence. The tough Navy contract not only included penalties but also required Grumman to develop and deliver anything from 722 down to 361 F-14s, depending on what the Navy wanted, over the entire period of the 1970s. All this for essentially a fixed price. That was fine, provided Grumman's predictions of cost continued to be correct. To allow for inflation, an annual three percent rise was permitted on labor and two percent on materials. In any case, Grumman had no way of knowing with any certainty what it would actually cost to develop the F-14 then

Venting fuel as it approaches the Long Island shoreline, the very first F-14 is seen with wings in the low-speed high-lift mode. Not many air-to-air pictures were taken of it, because it only flew twice, as explained on the facing page. Loss of this aircraft did not seriously hurt the program, however.

build it many years hence. What in fact happened was that Grumman's overall business declined, so the F-14 had to bear a higher proportion of the financial overheads. Much worse, inflation began to climb and soon went through the eight percent level.

No manufacturer could live with such a situation. Grumman told the Navy it could not deliver Lot 4 of production airplanes except at a loss. In January 1972 the company advised that it would lose $105 million on Lot 4, and that it would not accept Lot 5 or any further production batches without a new agreement. It was a time of immense stress during which Lew Evans suffered a heart attack that contributed to his death six months later. His replacement was Clint Towl. After further prolonged hassle, Towl agreed to build the 48 airplanes in Lot 5, thereby pushing up the company's total loss on F-14 manufacture to roughly $220 million, while in return the Navy agreed to a new repriced contract for Lot 6 onward. The company wanted to stay in business, and by this time the Navy knew the F-14 to be the best fighter in the world, and wanted that too. The restructured contract satisfied both parties, but while the situation was crucial there was no possibility of funding the F401 engine, and the airplane delivered to the Navy has been the F-14A right through to 1987.

It is not quite the original airplane, however. The most important change has certainly been Pratt & Whitney's progressive improvement of the TF30 engine. Its shortcomings really became manifest only after the F-14A's entry to regular service, which began with VF-1 and VF-2 in October 1972. As hours began to pile up, with ordinary squadron pilots working the throttles back and forth while pulling "g's" in simulated combat, failures occurred of which the most dangerous was a breakup of the fan (the enlarged first three stages of the low-pressure compressor). Accordingly the TF30-412 was modified into the Dash-414, with changes to the fan and a surrounding casing of strong steel so that, should a fan disintegrate, nothing would come through to cause dangerous damage to the aircraft. The fan blades themselves were made of improved titanium alloy. Changes were also made to the aircraft engine bays for improved safety and fire protection, and to enhance survivability of the flight controls. These modifications still left room for improvement and at the end of the 1970s Pratt & Whitney began modifying engines to Dash-414A standard giving better stall resistance, reliability and engine life.

The 1987 production engine, still suffered from many problems, a new one being that it leaves a smoky trail. By the late 1970s the Navy was forced to recognize that, in the words of Navy Secretary John F. Lehman, Jr., (himself a Naval Reserve flight officer), the engine/ airframe mismatch was "probably the worst we have had in many years" (the same thing was said by the Air Force about the TF30 in the F-111). Accordingly plans were made for an alternative engine, the General Electric F110, originally called the F101DFE (Derivative Fighter Engine). After careful ground testing, two DFEs were fitted into the seventh F-14 (No. 157986, previously the F-14B) and put through a flight test program in July–September 1981. Grumman had painted the legend "Super Tomcat" across the tails, and with the GE engine this is just what the F-14 had become. In July 1984 Grumman was awarded a $984 million contract for a long-term upgrade program, beginning with the F-14A (Plus) powered by the new engines but otherwise unchanged, and moving on to the F-14D with new engines and completely new radar and digital avionics.

So far all F-14A's have had similar systems and weapons. Standard internal fuel amounts to no less than 2,385 U.S. gallons which is sufficient for a four-hour endurance with ample reserves without having to use the inflight-refueling probe which can be extended from the right side of the nose. The aircraft can also carry 267-gallon drop tanks fitted under the engine pods. The radar is part of the giant Hughes AWG-9 fire-control system, able to detect air targets at ranges up to 195 miles according to their size and aspect, track 24 of them simultaneously and attack a selected six simultaneously. Armament is superior to that of any other fighter known, for it can include the AIM-54 Phoenix missile which can kill from ranges exceeding 100 miles, the AIM-7 Sparrow medium-range radar-guided missile (which relies on continuous illumination of the target by the missile's own radar), AIM-9 Sidewinder IR-homing close-range missiles and an internal M61 gun with 675 rounds of 20-mm ammunition. Four Phoenix or Sparrow missiles can be attached under the fuselage, the former on large interface pallets and the Sparrows recessed. Two more of each, or two pairs of Sidewinders, can be carried on cranked pylons under the fixed wing gloves, these being angled outboard to enable the main wheels to retract forward and upward between the missiles and fuselage. Provision is made for a total load of 14,500 pounds of ordnance

Even today the Hughes AWG-9 radar fire-control system is one of the most powerful and versatile fitted to any fighter, and teamed with the AIM-54 Phoenix missile it gives the F-14A a stand-off kill capability not even approached by any other Western fighter. With the radome raised to the vertical position for maintenance, the 36-in. planar-array antenna is completely exposed, while the main radar boxes are reached through access panels.

(bombs, missiles, rockets and other stores) in various surface-attack and antiship roles, but so far this has not been used despite the aerodynamic suitability of a swing-wing aircraft for dual roles. A total of 49 F-14s, as was, were allocated in 1980–81 to carry the Tactical Air Reconnaissance Pod System to enable them to replace the RF-8G and RA-5C in the carrier-based multisensor reconnaissance mission, for which no special-purpose aircraft has been procured. Thanks to the speed and range of the F-14, it was judged that these aircraft could fly reconnaissance missions while still retaining full armament capability. Each TARPS pod contains three sensors, a framing camera for forward

oblique or vertical photography, a panoramic (horizon-to-horizon) camera and an infra-red line scanner which creates a TV-type picture based on thermal differences in the scene. Another sensor becoming standard on the F-14A is the Northrop television camera set, which is housed in a prominent pod under the nose. It can search the sky in a wide-angle mode then switch to a high-magnification mode for positive identification of the target. Not only can the type of aircraft be identified but, in good conditions, it is even possible to check on the weapons it is carrying and thus know best how to select the right engagement tactics.

Few aircraft have ever been able to fight with more types of weapons than the F-14, and of course in carrying AIM-54 Phoenix this fighter is unique. Here (from the front) are: four AIM-9 Sidewinder AAMs (various subtypes), six AIM-7 Sparrow AAMs, and 20 mm ammunition for the M61A-1 gun, six AIM-54 Phoenix AAMs, two external fuel tanks, and various—bombs, including Snakeye retarded bombs and dispensers.

As the most advanced fighter in the world, the Tomcat was not initially thought of as an export proposition, particularly in view of its specialist naval nature and high price. In 1973, however, the Shah of Iran was looking for a fighter able to shoot down the Soviet MiG-25R Foxbat reconnaissance aircraft which were making frequent overflights beyond the reach of Iran's F-4 Phantoms. Money was no object, and after carefully evaluating everything on offer the Iranian Air Force picked the F-14A, signing for 30 in June 1974 and a further 50 in January 1975. Four years later the Shah was overthrown, and the 79 Tomcats already delivered became the top fighters of the Islamic Republic of Iran Air Force. They have been engaged from the start in the long war with neighbouring Iraq, but Grumman is specifically prohibited from offering field support, and F-14A serviceability is assumed to be low.

U.S. Navy F-14A Tomcats line up at Miramar Naval Air Station, California, home for a large number of fighter and airborne early warning units and one of the key West Coast centers of naval aviation.

Because of its amazingly futuristic design and unique fighting qualities, the F-14 has unquestionably survived its propulsion problems and emerged as one of the best and longest-lived of all the world's fighter aircraft. Indeed, in many respects its capabilities remain unique, more than 15 years after its first flight. To put the importance of this program into perspective, the F-14 today is as old as the F3F would have been in 1952, and the end of F-14 production will come well after the year 1963 in F3F terms.

But the F-14 is not the company's only long-lived program. The same can be said of its other big contributions to the U.S. Navy's carriers, the A-6 and its variants, and the E-2 and C-2. Production of the standard A-6E Intruder and A-6E TRAM (fitted with the Target Recognition and Attack Multisensor turret under the nose) continued through the 1970s, but by the mid-1980s was being upgraded to the A-6F, described in the next chapter. One version, the KA-6D, occupied the entire 1970s and bids fair to keep the company's St. Augustine division busy throughout the 1980s as well. All the KA-6D's are conversions of earlier Intruders, initially all A-6A's, for the primary role of carrier-based air refueling tanker. Early examples retained a capability for day ground attack and of managing a sea/air rescue operation, however the latest KA-6D's are dedicated tankers with no weapons or alternate mission role. Fuel is passed out through a hose drum unit recessed inside the rear fuselage, and the latest standard aircraft (to which earlier KA's are being converted) can carry five 400-gal. external tanks. Conversions totalled 78 from the A-6A, plus an initial 11 from the A-6E.

Above: A rare picture of Iranian F-14A Tomcats on a training mission, with wings and glove vanes ready for supersonic flight. Such a scene would be difficult to repeat today, because Mehrabad, Bushehr and Shiraz have only nominal aircraft at each base, and very few trained crews.

Opposite: Another unusual shot looking back at an F-14A of U.S. Navy fighter squadron VF-102 "Diamondbacks" heading out from its great floating base CV-66 *America*. It has the television camera set, two tanks, and Phoenix, Sparrow and Sidewinder AAMs.

Below: A Prowler is managed by an integrated four-man team. Their duties are outlined on the facing page.

Bottom: An EA-6B Prowler of VAQ-129 "New Vikings," the Whidbey Island training unit. All five tactical jamming pods are being carried, each powered by a windmill generator on its nose.

An even bigger A-6 program concerns the manufacture or conversion of aircraft for the EW (electronic warfare) role. This task began in 1963 when the Marine Corps drew up a requirement for an A-6 which, while retaining attack capability, could also carry an extensive internal passive receiver system to detect, locate, classify and record hostile radars (especially SAM guidance radars) and many other kinds of emission. This task was done by the EW aircraft initially called the A2F-1H and later EA-6A which carried a giant array of antennas in a fin-cap fairing, plus over 30 different antennas throughout the aircraft. Parts of the navigation and bombing avionics were removed, but full weapon-carrying capability remained. In the EW role, however, some or all of the pylons could be occupied by active jammer pods, each tuned to specific hostile wavebands. Each pod, resembling a drop tank, had a windmill on the nose driving an electric generator, and broadcast its jamming signals ahead and/or to the rear. Grumman converted 12 A-6s into EA's, followed by 15 built new, all for the Marines.

An EW Intruder was obviously needed by the Navy as well but in 1966 this service decided to go whole hog and procure a dedicated and truly capable aircraft for this role, eschewing all attack capability. The basic task was development of the advanced tactical jamming system, and the resulting ALQ-99 was produced by the Air Borne Instrument Co. Hostile signals are sensed and processed as before in the antenna

group located inside the giant fin cap made by Canadair. The resulting information is fed to a central computer and made available to the four crew members. The crew includes a pilot seated on the left in front, and three ECMOs (ECM Officers). Two ECMOs seated in the rear manage the ALQ-99 system, and the ECMO beside the pilot handles navigation, communications, defensive ECM and chaff dispensing. A total of ten jamming transmitters can be carried in five external pods, each with its own integral windmill generator. To handle the considerably increased normal operating weights of this version, the EA-6B Prowler, the wings and some other parts of primary structure are strengthened or reinforced, and the engines are changed to the J52-408 version rated at 11,200 pounds of thrust.

Prowlers had no attack capability, but in 1986 the AGM-88A HARM (High-speed Anti-Radar Missile) was introduced on wing pylons. Prowler deliveries began in 1971, and in 1987 the Navy VAQ squadrons were almost up to strength, though it is planned to deliver 12 new aircraft per year until at least 1989. All in service are being upgraded with major new avionics items which will greatly enhance operational capability, improve self-defense and permit carrier recoveries to be made in zero-zero weather.

Top: Maintenance on the deck of USS *Enterprise* for an EA-6B of VAQ-134 "Garudas" in the Pacific.

Designation: EA-6B PROWLER
Type: Carrier-based electronic countermeasures.
Powerplant: Two Pratt & Whitney J52-P-408 turbojets, 11,200 lb. thrust each.
Wingspan: 53 ft. 0 in.
Length: 59 ft. 10 in.
Height: 16 ft. 3 in (15ft. 6 in loaded)
Weight: 58,000 lb.
Maximum Speed: 651 mph at sea level.
Ceiling: 41,200 ft.
Range: 1,099 miles; max. external fuel 2,399 miles.
Crew: 4.
Users: USN, USMC.

In the previous chapter it was explained how Grumman took a considerable risk in launching the G-159 Gulfstream I twin-turboprop executive aircraft. In fact, this program showed a profit on all airplanes from No. 22 to 200, and well into the 1960s there was no problem in finding customers. But Grumman naturally looked far ahead, and in the longer term it could see that executive jets would make life increasingly difficult for the slower turboprop. In 1963 the decision was made to plan a corporate jet aircraft. Though initially it might appear to compete with the Gulfstream I, the GII (Gulfstream II) was a success from the start, about 60 being spoken for before the first was delivered. Rather larger than the GI, and quite different in appearance, the GII has swept wings, a lofty T-tail and two Rolls-Royce Spey turbofan engines hung on the sides of the rear fuselage. As before, Grumman aimed at the absolute top end of the market, creating a literal Rolls-Royce of the skies, with transcontinental or transoceanic range carrying (typically) eight passengers in sumptuous comfort at nearly 600 mph at 43,000 ft. With more seats it carries up to 19 passengers.

The first GII flew on October 2, 1966, after a very quick design program, and deliveries began at the end of 1967. In July 1975, at aircraft No. 166, Grumman introduced hush kits to make the Spey engines more environmentally acceptable (there was never any problem with noise in the cabin), and in the same year testing began of the first GII with long-range tanks in the outer wings. Conflict between marketing the GII and the earlier GI was almost non-existent, and with hindsight it appears that the move into jets was made at exactly the right time. The GII in fact outsold the GI before itself being succeeded by today's GIII and GIV, 256 being completed by January 1, 1980.

Below: The shapely Gulfstream II, known as the "G II" to the aviation fraternity, was even more of a financial gamble than its turbo-prop predecessor. It was also an even greater success. It can truly be called the Rolls-Royce of business jets. RR makes the engines; and the British company also owns this particular GII.

For sound reasons Grumman eased the Gulfstream business away from its mainstream operations at Bethpage. First it sought a totally new high-tech manufacturing plant, and this was built at Savannah, Georgia, formally opening on September 29, 1967. GII's came off two assembly lines as "green airplanes", which were subsequently flown to completion centers for outfitting to the customer's specification with avionics, interior furnishings and exterior paint trim. Two years later, in 1969, the now large and rather unwieldy Grumman split itself into a parent Grumman Corporation with four operating subsidiaries. In the early 1970s the number of subsidiaries grew to seven, an entirely new one being Grumman American Aviation Corporation. This had one foot in the Gulfstream program and the other in a tiny two-seat lightplane, the Bede BD-1, notable for its metal-bonded construction. This was developed by American Aviation Corporation, formed for this purpose in 1964, and went into production in 1968 at a small plant next to Cuyahoga County Airport, Cleveland, Ohio. The range of AAC products burgeoned, and in the early 1970s AAC was picked by Grumman as a target for its planned move into the field of general aviation. A full merger became effective on January 1, 1973. For a while the company's executive offices were at Cleveland, but the main plant continued to be at Savannah, where both the GII jets and the lightplanes were built.

Further change was to come. Grumman chose to divest itself of the general-aviation business, and on September 1, 1978, it was announced that Grumman American had been sold to American Jet Industries, a California-based company which ultimately changed its name to Gulfstream Aerospace, with corporate offices at Savannah. It has been there ever since, busily building a wide range of light aircraft, the GII and new GIII. As part of the deal, Grumman completed development of the GIII, a GII with more fuel and new wings of increased aerodynamic efficiency. The GIII first flew on December 2, 1979, and Grumman received a royalty on the first 200 GIIIs sold after January 1, 1980.

Above: The prototype of the Grumman American GA-7 Cougar shows the attractive lines of this four-seater, powered by twin 160-horsepower Lycoming engines. The pitot installation on the right wingtip was special test instrumentation, fitted for the first flight on December 20, 1974.

The Shuttle 41-D mission at the point of igniting main engines on Pad A at Kennedy Complex 39 in June 1984. Grumman played a major role in the basic configuration of the Shuttle Orbiter and has made all the wings.

When the company restructured in 1969, the operating company responsible for its mainstream airplane business was announced as Grumman Aerospace Corporation. It remained a prosperous and well-founded operation, though in the early 1970s there was no certainty that the biggest programs – the F-14, A-6, E-2 and derivatives – would go on through 1990. Moreover, all were for the Navy, and as Grumman wanted a broader customer base it set about building up a large and growing business making major parts for other people's airplanes. The plant at Milledgeville, Georgia, went to work making fiberglass wingtips for the Fairchild A-10A Thunderbolt II attack aircraft (while Fairchild made vertical tails for Grumman's F-14). In 1978 Grumman won a contract to make major parts of the Sikorsky CH-53E helicopter, and at the end of the decade, when Boeing began manufacturing the 767 jetliner, it announced that Grumman Aerospace would make the wing center section, an adjacent lower fuselage section and fuselage bulkheads.

Back in 1974 Grumman had received a design study contract for a special rebuild of the F-111A for tactical electronic warfare missions. This very important airplane, the EF-111A Raven, is described in the next chapter. Right at the end of the decade, Grumman received a $3 million contract from Defense Advanced Research Projects Agency for design and wind tunnel testing of models for possible FSW (forward-swept wing) airplanes.

Diversification

Previous page: The Grumman X-29A forward swept wing aircraft is one of the most exciting shapes in the sky. A collaborative program by the Defense Advanced Research Projects Agency, USAF and NASA, it could revolutionize the design of all high-speed airplanes. Grumman built two of these amazing research vehicles, the first flown on December 14, 1984, and the No. 2 scheduled to fly in 1988.

Had Grumman been told in 1970 that it would enter the year 1988 without having won a single major new aircraft program since the F-14, it would have been very worried indeed. The management might have been more than a little incredulous had they been assured that, despite this, the shop floor would be full of work, there would be few layoffs, and the future would look as bright as ever!

The chief reason for the lack of a new program is the excellence of the existing products. Almost without precedent, the A-6 and E-2, both designed in the 1950s, remain in full production and improved versions will continue to be built. The great F-14, which in 1973 appeared due for imminent termination, will continue in production into the 1990s. Nobody could have foreseen this when the F-14 was being designed. It certainly does not mean the U.S. is crippled by budget restrictions, or is simply buying obsolescent airplanes. What it does mean is that the team that conceived the original F-14 did such a brilliant job of designing it to accommodate future growth that, even today and in the increasingly perilous skies of the 1990s, the Tomcat will still defeat any challenger.

Going back to the mid-1970s, the Navy and Marines did seek a new NACF (Navy Air Combat Fighter). It looked then as if the F-14 would be too expensive to replace the F-4 on a one-for-one basis, and the NACF was planned as a smaller, lightweight airplane which could replace the F-4 in the fighter mission and the A-7 in the attack mission.

Grumman had no chance to win the NACF program because Congress decreed that the Navy should choose a version of one of the USAF lightweight fighters. The choice fell on the F/A-18 Hornet, derived jointly by McDonnell Douglas and Northrop from the latter's YF-17. But in any event this aircraft proved to be priced at almost the same level as the F-14; moreover, its short range in the attack mission and its limited all-weather attack capability has resulted in a 1987 decision to alter the basic mix of airplanes in each carrier air wing. In the future, four F-14s, four F/A-18s and four KA-6D tankers will be withdrawn from each wing. In their place will come ten more A-6 Intruders and one more EA-6B Prowler and one more E-2C Hawkeye – every one a Grumman product.

Even before this far-reaching decision, the A-6 was very much an ongoing program. The original A-6's have long since been updated to later models, and from 1987 on, every A-6 built for the Navy and Marine Corps is expected to be fitted with new graphite/epoxy composite wings. The new wings will clear new aircraft for 8,800 hours of combat flying at high weights. Retrofit aircraft will have an extended service life depending upon their individual remaining fuselage life. In parallel, under a major contract awarded in 1984, Grumman is developing a completely new second-generation Intruder designated the A-6F. It is expected that all future A-6 production will be of this type; existing A-6E's could be reworked to the same standard, but as this book went to press no decision has been made concerning the future mix of new and reworked aircraft.

The list of improvements in the A-6F is a long one, and altogether the new aircraft will have its mission effectiveness multiplied. For a start, it has new engines. In place of the J52 turbojets, the A-6F will have two General Electric F404-GE-400D turbofans. These are basically the same engine as fitted to the F/A-18 Hornet but without afterburner. The result is an engine roughly the same size as the J52 but much lighter,

Left: Grumman employees reconditioning an A-6E at the St. Augustine facility in Florida.

The A-6F engineering mockup at Calverton played a central role not only by helping Grumman engineers to solve the spatial problems but also by making everything highly visible in order to facilitate discussion with the customer. Not the least remarkable thing about this long-lived Grumman program is that the first Mock-up Review Board for the first A-6 (then called Grumman G-128 and later the A2F-1) was held at Bethpage *twenty-nine years earlier.*

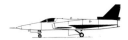

more powerful (10,800 lb. instead of 9,300 lb. thrust) and with improved fuel economy. The fuel system has also been upgraded, with self-sealing armored pipelines and fire-protection foam filling the voids between the airframe and the tanks, and new fire-detection sensors have been located throughout the aircraft.

The leading edge of the wing root is redesigned with an extended slat and a redesigned fillet similar to that fitted to the EA-6B Prowler. On the latter, the aerodynamics were improved to permit operation at higher gross weight, but on the A-6F the objective was to give better lift on carrier landings. Thus, at lighter weights the landing speed will be reduced by up to 12 mph, reducing stress on the main gears. In turn this will enable the weight limit for carrier landings to be increased from 36,000 lb. to 38,400 lb. The severe 36,000 lb. restriction caused thousands of costly bombs and missiles to be dumped into the ocean to get the aircraft's weight below the limit. With the A-6F this will no longer be necessary.

From the point of view of maintenance, the new engines are certain to bring a giant improvement. Moreover, the numerous engine-driven accessories, gearbox and drive are all mounted not on the engine but on the airframe. Thus, should it be necessary to change an engine, all that

Below: Grumman rolls out the first A-6F Intruder at Calverton on August 31 1987.

need be done is uncouple the engine's own fuel and control connections then pull the engine out, leaving the complex accessory section in place. Another big plus is the addition of a gas-turbine auxiliary power unit, making the new Intruder independent of yellow service carts.

Probably the most important improvements concern the vital mission avionics and cockpit. Much of the new equipment will be common to that of the forthcoming F-14D Tomcat. One item peculiar to the A-6F is a totally new Norden multimode radar, operating in the 16GHz frequency band. Among its many advanced features are an air/air combat mode, doppler beam sharpening for high resolution ground mapping, an inverse synthetic-aperature mode for classifying ship targets from long distances, increased range for target recognition,

Below right: The A-6F Intruders first flight. This, the first of five full scale development aircraft, will be used to test various aerodynamic improvements, such as the wing root extensions, and the new General Electric F404-GE-400D engine.

acquisition and tracking, with standoff weapon capability, and better reliability and maintainability. The new radar will accommodate the range of the latest AGM-84D Harpoon cruise missile and future stand-off missiles to be carried by all A-6 aircraft.

To match the vastly enhanced flow of information from the new radar, the entire cockpit of the A-6F has been redesigned. Five new multifunction displays face the crew, each with surrounding buttons for changing the menu or the scale of picture or managing various other functions. The pilot has comprehensive vertical and horizontal situation displays, the former backing up the advanced Kaiser head-up display which replaces the A-6E's.

While the doppler navigation radar previously fitted is absent from the A-6F, the new model will have greater navigation accuracy from the ASN-130 inertial system. Other new avionics include twin AYK-14 tactical computers, ASW-27 two-way secure data link, ALR-67 radar warning system, the ALQ-165 airborne self-protection jammer, improved tactical software, and a common air-data computer. All avionics are linked into a digital data bus, which is extended to include weapon pylons for the Harpoon, Maverick and HARM missiles, and new outer-wings pylons for self-defense Sidewinder or AMRAAM missiles.

Since 1985, Grumman has been building five development proto-types of the A-6F, which were scheduled to fly in August and November 1987, and February, April and June 1988. Production deliveries are scheduled to begin in 1990. The Navy's original total requirement for the F amounted to 150 aircraft by calendar year 1995, but with the reconfigured composition of the carrier air wings this total is likely to increase. It is quite possible this evergreen medium-attack airplane will still be in production at the end of the century. And Grumman is even now defining a similar major upgrade for the EA-6B Prowler.

Below: Externally hard to distinguish from any other F-14, apart from engine nozzles and paint scheme, this long-serving development airplane is actually the first of the new breed of Tomcat with more power and fewer problems. As explained on the facing page, its new engines give tomorrow's F-14s even greater all-round flight performance.

Mention has already been made of the F-14D Tomcat. The millions who have seen the film "Top Gun" may think there is little wrong with today's F-14A, and there is not a man in the Navy who would disagree with the statement, "It's a *great* airplane!" The fact remains, as explained earlier, that the basically superb fighter has always suffered from propulsion difficulties, and this was the most urgent problem addressed by Grumman with the F-14A (Plus). It will be recalled from an earlier chapter that the TF30 was never intended to be more than an interim engine, and back in 1973 a prototype F-14 flew with the F401 engine which was envisioned as the powerplant of the F-14B and F-14C. But this augmented turbofan program was cancelled and the B and C models remained stillborn. Something had to be done, however, and eventually the Navy, like the Air Force, turned to General Electric's outstanding F101DFE (Derivative Fighter Engine). Two of these performed brilliantly in F-14A No. 157986, which bore the legend "Super Tomcat" on its tails, between July and September 1981. Not only did the new engines deliver power of a totally new order, with maximum thrust at takeoff increased from the 20,900 lb. level up to 27,600 lb. (a very conservative rating), but at last it freed the pilot from all concern in connection with the engines. The new GE engine was found to behave impeccably under the worst conditions the pilot could contrive, giving what is popularly called carefree handling. It also promised excellent reliability, for in its many prototype test programs (not only in the F-14) the F101DFE never needed an engine change or even a trial run.

Accordingly GE developed this engine into a fully-engineered fighter powerplant, now in production in different versions for the Air Force and Navy as the F110. The initial Navy production engine is the F110-400, and by mid-1987 Grumman was to have two development aircraft flying with these engines as part of the F-14A+ program. The A+ airplane is essentially unchanged except for the new engine.

Above: Back in 1973 the seventh F-14A prototype, No. 157986, was flown with F401 engines as the proposed F-14B. Today it is continuing its work as the Super Tomcat with new General Electric F110 engines.

Left: Such is the progress in engine design that, despite its far greater power and other advantages, the General Electric F110 augmented turbofan is actually very much smaller and lighter than the TF30-P-414A used in the F-14A. The highly reliable F110-GE-400 completely transforms the performance capabilities of the F-14A (Plus) and F-14D

Above: Looking pristine in glossy white paint, at Grumman's Calverton plant, the first F-14A (Plus) gradually takes shape. Between the empty engine bays can be seen the open airbrakes; in the background a crane has just replaced the canopy.

Grumman expects to deliver a total of 70 new and remanufactured F-14A (Plus) aircraft from fiscal year 1987 through fiscal year 1990.

As noted earlier, Grumman is now working flat out on a much bigger update program, creating the F-14D. Initially funded under a long-term $984 million fixed-price contract signed in July 1984, this will at last result in what can fairly be called the definitive Tomcat, which will combine the new engines with totally upgraded avionics, weapons and equipment. Even then, so right was the original F-14, it is difficult to find many external differences between the D-model and the very first Tomcat of 1972.

Basically, the F-14D changes over from outdated analog avionics to the far superior digital kind, with almost every functioning item in the aircraft tied to a digital bus (a major data highway able to convey millions of items of data each second). The new digital systems will replace about two-thirds of the F-14's numerous avionics boxes, providing new sensors, weapons management, navigation displays and control functions.

The largest single item is, of course, the main radar which fills the nose. Though derived from the existing AWG-9, the new Hughes AN/APG-71 radar will be in many respects the most powerful and capable fitted to any fighter. Its many advanced features include monopulse angle tracking, digital scan control, target identification (including non-cooperative targets), and raid assessment by counting numbers of hostile aircraft. It will be able to counter sophisticated enemy electronic countermeasures by means of a low-sidelobe antenna

and sidelobe-blanking guard channel, frequency agility (the ability to hop rapidly and randomly from one operating frequency to another) and a new high-speed digital signal processor. The digital bus will also integrate the Litton ALR-67 threat-warning and recognition system, the Westinghouse/ITT ALQ-165 airborne self-protection jammer, which under computer control helps the aircraft survive in hostile airspace, the joint tactical information distribution system, and an infra-red search and track sensor and television camera set which can "see" hostile aircraft clearly at a distance of scores of miles. Throughout there is a lot of commonality with the A-6F and F/A-18.

The F-14D will accommodate its pilot and radar intercept officer on Martin-Baker Navy aircrew common ejection seats, which are not only comfortable but have computer control to match their ejection power and trajectory to the particular mass distribution of the human occupant. The M61 gun is retained, and studies are under way to upgrade the missile fit.

One of the 1987 development prototypes is being completed to full F-14D standard, and three more will be used, together with a EA-3B Skywarrior, for radar and avionics development. The first F-14D for the inventory is scheduled to be delivered in March 1990.

A full force of production and retrofit F-14D aircraft will be in service by the late 1990s.

It has previously been explained how Grumman became associate contractor for the Navy version of the General Dynamics F-111. Once this difficult episode had been terminated, in 1968, Grumman expected

Above: Seen from above, the first of the new GE-engined Tomcats looks even more complicated. The actual wing pivots can be seen (normally they are covered by a flush-fitting panel) and when this picture was taken the canopy and ejection seats were absent, to facilitate work in the cockpits.

that it would never have much to do with the F-111 again. In fact in the 1970s Grumman began a wholly new involvement with these big swing-wing airplanes, and this time the association has been a happy one.

The Vietnam war brought home to the USAF the fact that there was no land-based dedicated electronic countermeasures airplane to equal the carrier-based EA-6B Prowler. True, the sturdy old EB-66 converted bombers had done a good job, but they were primitive and vulnerable. What was needed was an airplane as fast and technically modern as the front-line USAF attack airplanes, able to fly with them – deep into enemy territory if necessary – creating invisible screens of jamming radio power over vast areas of sky to help the attackers get through. A further requirement was to receive, analyze and evaluate hostile radio and radar emissions of all kinds. In the close air support role, the new airplane would be needed to neutralize enemy anti-air radars and SAM systems, often from quite close range, though it was not required to carry anti-radar missiles, which is the job of the Advanced Wild Weasel series of airplanes, such as the F-4G.

Clearly the Air Force could order a completely new aircraft for this vital task, but that would be very expensive and take many years.

Alternatively it might meet the requirement by modifying existing airplanes, but this would be a major challenge because the reconstruction would have to be total. After most careful research and study, the Air Force agreed with General Dynamics and Grumman that the best solution would be to rebuild available F-111A attack airplanes to carry the ALQ-99E electronic tactical jamming system. In 1974 study contracts were awarded to the two companies. In January 1975 Grumman received the first contract for hardware, $85.9 million for conversion of two aircraft to service as protypes of the EF-111A Raven. The first of these flew as a complete operative system for the first time on May 17, 1977, and the first Raven for the USAF inventory was delivered in November 1981. Grumman converted a total force of 42 Air Force F-111s to the electronic countermeasures EF-111A configuration, all of which were delivered by the summer of 1985. In the 1970s, the original Air Force analysis showed a need for 90 EF-111s. The aircraft's role in the raid on Libya has increased the interest in continuing the program, and the Air Force is expected to buy additional EF-111s as soon as its budget permits. Grumman will compete aggressively for this business.

The photograph on these pages shows the so-called "aerodynamic prototype" of the EF-111A Raven, which first flew on March 10, 1977. Distinguished by its fin-tip pod and underbelly radome, USAF No 66-049 was aerodynamically almost an EF-111A though it lacked the actual avionics systems.

One of the crucial factors making the conversion possible is the fact that the ALQ-99E, though hailed as the world's most powerful airborne ECM system, does not require the addition of two extra crew members, as in the EA-6B. Instead the entire mission workload, which in the Navy airplane needs three men, is handled by the lone electronic warfare officer seated to the right of the pilot. This is especially important in the F-111, because the two crew members occupy a unique capsule which, in emergency, is ejected from the aircraft as a single unit. It would have been difficult and costly to add two extra electronic warfare officers. The answer was to reduce crew workload by increased automation, and the ALQ-99E is preprogrammed with a vast library of almost every enemy emitter the EF-111A is likely to encounter.

Grumman subcontracted the work on the fin (vertical stabilizer) to Canadair in Montreal. This surface carries a giant streamlined pod, outwardly resembling that of the EA-6B, within which are grouped the receivers and antennae. Within the fuselage are power systems and management equipment, cooling systems and all necessary computers. The powerful and versatile jamming transmitters, which in the EA-6B are housed in external underwing pods, are permanently installed in the weapons bay. The antennae are carried in a row under the airplane's belly, where they are faired-in by what is aptly called a canoe radome, some 16 ft. (4.9 m) in length. Total weight of the new electronics in the EF-111A is about three tons.

The EF-111A program represented a very great challenge, carried through with complete success. In service these complex machines equip the 42nd and 390th Electronic Combat Squadrons of the U.S. Air Force, the former being part of the 20th Tactical Fighter Wing based at

RAF Upper Heyford in England. Extensive tests have confirmed that the EF-111A has the performance to fly in formation with the latest fighter and attack aircraft if necessary; it is described as handling very much like a regular F-111 with a bombload. Other tests have confirmed that it can do its job of jamming enemy radars and other emitters while causing no interference to the vital electronics of friendly aircraft (which may be very close to it). The Air Force is now engaged in a major update, costing about $200 million, to equip these vital aircraft to meet new threats and provide enhanced capabilities against early-warning radars, ground control of interception systems and SAM acquisition radars.

Work continues on a five-year, $109 million contract signed in 1986 for the avionics modernization of 152 Air Force aircraft. Grumman and teammate TRW are updating the navigation and communications systems of General Dynamics F-111A's and F-111E's, and Grumman EF-111A's.

Far left top: EF-111A with wings at 72.5^0 sweep.

Far left center: The giant fin pod houses the group of receiver antennae.

Far left bottom: A combat-ready Raven of the 42nd ECS based in England.

Below: A U.S. Air Force Raven, the British-based aircraft which cooperated in the successful operation against Libya in 1986, returns to Upper Heyford.

Above: Raven maintenance at RAF Upper Heyford. The giant duct between wing and tail houses the avionics refrigeration radiator.

Right: A Grumman tech rep checks an EF-111A test station at Upper Heyford.

Designation: EF-111A RAVEN.
Type: Electronic countermeasures.
Powerplant: Two Pratt & Whitney TF30-P-3 turbofans, 18,500 lb thrust each.
Wingspan: 63 ft. 0 in. (unswept), 31 ft. 11 in (swept).
Length: 76 ft. 0 in.
Height: 20 ft. 0 in.
Weight: 88,948 lb.
Maximum Speed: 1,377 mph.
Ceiling: 45,000 ft.
Range: Combat radius 230-929 miles.
Crew: 2.
Users: USAF

Another airplane developed in the fifties is the E-2 Hawkeye. For many years the standard production version has been the E-2C, and Grumman is continuing to build new examples at about the rate of six per year, and will go on doing so into the 1990s. By 1987 the company had delivered 106 Hawkeyes to the Navy, with an additional 22 on firm order. In addition, smaller numbers have been supplied to Israel, Japan, Egypt and Singapore, and several other countries have negotiated for these costly but vital aircraft. A number of these potential customers have visited the Israeli air force, the Heyl Ha'Avir, to learn how the Hawkeye has kept watch over all the many hostile airbases which surround that country, especially in Syria, and when necessary has guided Israeli fighter and attack aircraft so that they have the best chance of destroying the enemy, or hitting their targets, and returning to base undamaged. The E-2C can handle all air, land and sea targets and traffic within a volume of three million cubic miles.

Grumman has both continued to build Hawkeyes and also to update the existing aircraft. The biggest single improvements have been the installation of a succession of new main radars, and even the APS-125 – which seemed the last word when it was introduced in the E-2C – has now given way to the APS-138, first fitted in 1983. A feature of the new radar is a totally new TRAC-A (total radiation aperture control antenna) to reduce sidelobes and overcome more sophisticated kinds of enemy jamming.

Late in 1986 the Navy began flight tests of an E-2 with new APS-145 radar hardware and software. This system lets the operators track more targets at greater ranges, and is better able to separate target information from ground clutter. The improvements also enable the system to avoid the effects of jamming. The APS-145 is expected to go into production aircraft before the end of 1988. For the more distant future Grumman has a $14 million Navy contract to test the first large conformal radar to fly, together with its associated microprocessor control. A conformal radar is one whose antennae conform to the shape of the airplane, and thus cause no additional aerodynamic drag. In the case of the E-2C the antennae are being installed along the leading edges of the wings and tail surfaces, and along the sides of the fuselage. The new installation serves as a very advanced anti-jamming ECM system.

Top: An E-2C comes in to hit *JFK's* No. 3 wire, and above: the Hawkeye is parked prior to being taken down to the hangars.

Left: Vortices stream behind the propellers as the catapult begins to hurl a Hawkeye of VAW-126 down the deck of *John F. Kennedy.*

For the even more distant future, Grumman is developing air early warning technologies that could be used by the Navy or Air Force – because the next major air early warning program may very well be used by both services. The platforms will be different. The Air Force will probably use a wide-bodied aircraft, while the Navy will integrate the same system into a smaller, more rugged airframe for use on carriers.

Grumman delivered 19 C-2A Greyhound COD (carrier on-board delivery) transports when the design was new, in the 1960s, and is now (in 1985-89) engaged in building a further 39 to complete the Navy's requirement. It has been shown that by placing a large multi-year contract, defense equipment can be purchased for significantly less money, quite apart from eliminating the price-hiking effect of inflation. Moreover, the Navy is getting upgraded airplanes. The new Greyhounds have more powerful engines, a more comfortable cabin, an auxiliary power unit to make the airplane independent of ground servicing and starting power, updated avionics and improved materials and coatings to resist corrosion.

Right: Five of the first G-111 Albatross rebuilds are in use with Chalks International, Resorts International's commuter carrier. These versatile amphibians cruise at about 186 mph. A projected turboprop version would cost more but be faster, though speed is not usually important.

The very first job the company ever did was to rework an old amphibian, and Grumman can still earn income from almost the same kind of work. The amphibian is the evergreen Albatross, many of which still exist, with substantial flight time left in their airframes. Grumman believes there is a market for Albatrosses updated and converted into civil transports, for commuter and holiday airlines and for corporate owners. Grumman gathered up 57 of the tough birds after Resorts International requested the redesign, then purchased the first 12 conversions.

Grumman flew the prototype conversion on February 13, 1979, and FAA certification was gained on April 29, 1980. The first "production" type conversion, designated as a Grumman G-111 Albatross, was completed in January 1984. Each rebuild involves a total inspection of the aircraft, with replacement of any structural parts needed to "zero-life" the airframe. Among other changes, the four capstrips of the wing center-section are all replaced by new strips of titanium. The engines are overhauled and new autofeathering and fire-detection/extinguishing systems added. The main door on the left and the emergency hatch on the right are replaced by new doors opening outward. Two new doors have been added forward, and the main door now has drop-down steps. The cabin is completely refurnished, with 28 passenger seats, a rear toilet and a station for a flight attendant. Many of the avionics items are replaced by new lightweight solid-state boxes, including RCA WeatherScout 2 radar faired into the nose (the original radar projected as a "thimble").

Grumman has various further ideas for Albatross conversions. One is a water bomber for fighting forest fires. Another would be powered by Garrett TPE331-15 turboprops driving quiet and efficient Dowty Rotol four-blade propellers.

Below: Two contrasting Grumman products on the deck of *JFK*: an A-6E and a C-2A Greyhound about to be catapulted off.

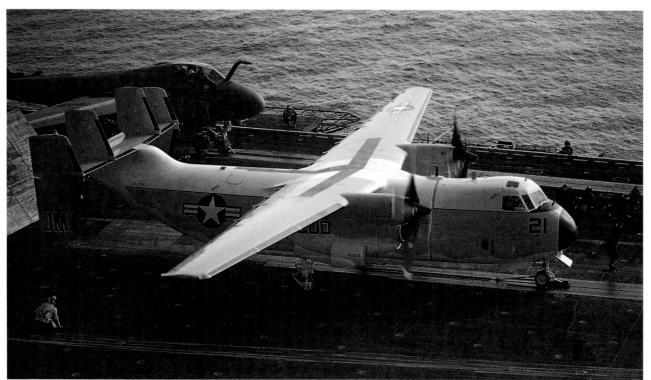

Until the 1980s Grumman had concentrated on production airplanes, and had never designed one intended purely for research. Perhaps there is more money in series production, but occasionally an opportunity comes along which can put a company even further out in front in the latest technology and could have an influence on winning future production awards. Just such an airplane is the X-29, though the uninitiated might be forgiven for thinking Grumman had fixed the tailfin on the nose and installed the pilot seat facing to the rear! The aircraft looks quite unique because the horizontal control surfaces are on the nose and the wings are swept sharply *forward*.

Sweeping the wings forward confers many benefits. Aerodynamic drag can be reduced at all speeds, especially near the speed of sound. For any given performance and capability a forward swept wing airplane can be made smaller, which means lighter, needing a smaller engine burning less fuel, which again reduces weight. A forward swept wing can give better lift at low speeds, making for slower and safer (and shorter) takeoff and landing. The airplane can be made virtually spin-proof, and its handling at low speeds can be almost perfect. The reason all fast jets have not been of the forward swept wing type is that until recently such a wing could not be built light enough, yet stiff enough to

Designation: X-29.
Type: Experimental forward swept wing demonstrator.
Powerplant: General Electric F404-GE-400 turbofan 16,000 lb.
Wingspan: 27 ft. 2½ in.
Length: 53 ft. 11¼ in.
Height: 14 ft. 3½ in.
Weight: 17,800 lb.
Maximum Speed: 1,060 mph.
Ceiling: About 55,000 ft.
Range: About 500 miles.
Crew: 1.

survive high speed flight. Aerodynamic forces would twist it, and as it twisted its angle would increase, greatly increasing the forces. (This phenomenon is called structural divergence.) In a split second the wing would be torn off.

In 1975, Col. Norris Krone Jr. of the U.S. Air Force showed how an FSW could be built, using modern composite materials such as carbon-fiber, structurally tailored to resist the brutal forces and still be light in weight. Nobody took up the idea. Then Krone got a call from a Grumman engineer, Glenn L. Spacht. He had independently discovered that the FSW gave lowest drag, and Krone's appeared to be the only confirming literature. To cut a long story short, on December 22, 1981, Grumman received an $80 million contract from the Defense Advanced Research Projects Agency to design, build and test two forward swept wing aircraft, designated X-29. To save money, the front end was taken from a Northrop F-5 light fighter, the main gears from an F-16, and many other items were bought off the shelf. The amazing wing was totally new, swept forward on the quarter-chord line at nearly 34°, yet very thin, stiff and strong with the fibers of carbon arranged in such directions that no catastrophic structural divergence can occur. Other new features include the canard foreplanes, the long rear inboard portion of each wing terminating with a trailing-edge flap like an elevator. Above all is the fast-acting computerized control system which, 40 times every second, corrects the flight of what is actually a highly unstable airplane.

Right: The first X-29 in final control system testing, prior to ground tests. Even though parts of other airplanes were used to save time and cost, the overall design and engineering effort was tremendous. Biggest of the development tasks was perfecting the hardware and software of the triple redundant flight-control computers, without which this amazingly unstable airplane could not fly.

Far right: When Grumman unveiled the first X-29 there were still doubters who were convinced it would be uncontrollable. So far the doubters have been confounded and the world's first supersonic FSW (forward swept wing) airplane has performed as predicted – brilliantly.

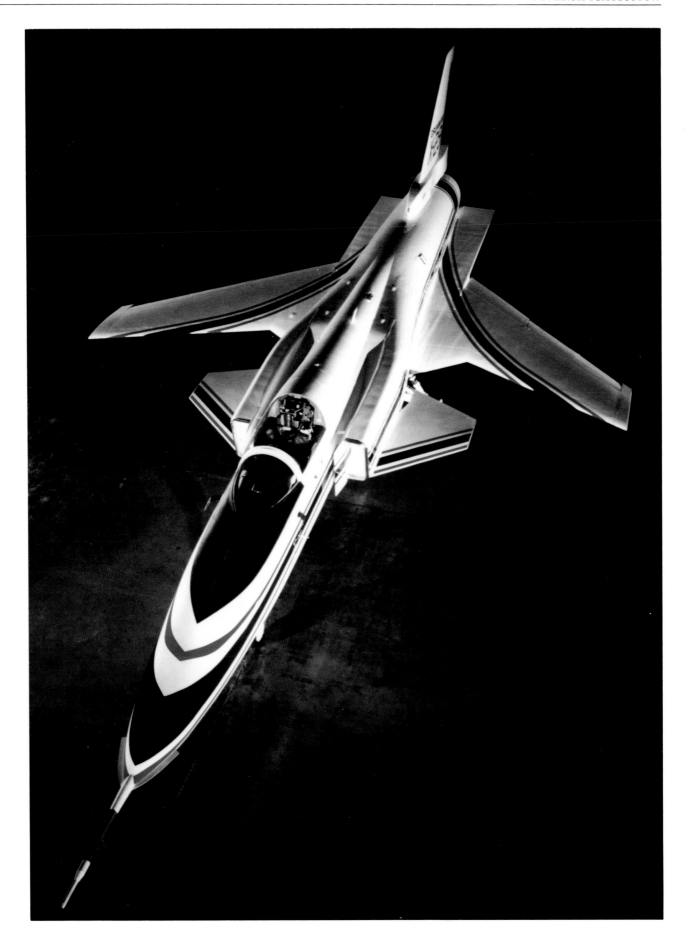

But before it ever flew, Grumman engineers left no questions unanswered concerning the X-29s controllability, airworthiness and pilot safety.

The use of computer models and analyses reduced wind-tunnel testing on the X-29 by about 10 percent compared to other new aircraft. A radio-controlled scale model built and flown in 1977 verified the computer codes. As the program progressed, a 1/8-scale wind-tunnel model was tested subsonically, transonically and supersonically at angles of attack as high as 90 degrees. Model force, moment, and pressure data were acquired from a 1/2-scale structural wing model.

During the develoment phase of the X-29, various structural element tests were conducted to evaluate materials and structural combinations. Full-scale structural tests were conducted on the flight vehicle. The X-29 was installed in a test fixture and simulated aerodynamic loads were imposed on the fuselage, wings, and control surfaces using hydraulic jacks. The tests verified that all structural design strength and aeroelastic tailoring characteristics of the X-29 were met or exceeded.

Tests were conducted on the plane itself and on a laboratory model housed in Grumman's Bethpage, New York, facility. The entire digital and analog X-29 flight control system underwent extensive laboratory testing. Simulators allowed pilots to experience realistic flight conditions. A hybrid simulation computer used a mathematical model of the X-29s flight characteristics to operate the laboratory's flight control

Below: During the takeoff and first flight of the X-29, chief test pilot Chuck Sewell remained a cool professional in control of this radically designed, unproven aircraft. The first flight was a complete success, and Sewell said that if the aircraft could be refueled immediately, he was ready and willing to take it for a second pass over the California desert.

system. Intensive testing was conducted using multiple failures, severe maneuvers, and flight outside the design envelope.

Another systems development tool was the total in-flight simulator. Full X-29 flight controls were fitted in a separate cockpit extending from the nose of an Air Force C-131B aircraft. Using this simulator, pilots were able to experience hands-on control responses using the fly-by-wire flight control systems with varying software modifications.

In other ground tests, hydraulic pressures of the X-29s actuators and other components were monitored by the X-29 hydraulic test stand.

The X-29 was already one of the most thoroughly tested aircraft before it ever left the ground.

Few first flights have been awaited with such eager anticipation as that of the radical and potentially tricky X-29. Tricky not because it had an FSW but because, like all modern fighter-type airplanes, it was deliberately made unstable in order to maneuver more rapidly. At last Grumman's chief test pilot, Charles A. "Chuck" Sewell, made the first flight at NASA's Dryden Research Center in California on December 14, 1984. Everything went fine. On subsequent flights the speed was gradually built up, other pilots took turns, and soon the X-29 was flying faster than sound. In 1988 the No. 2 airplane is scheduled to start a program of high angle of attack testing which will place the most severe stresses on the radical forward swept wing. As this book was written, all the evidence indicated that the forward swept wing was a winner.

Above: Chuck Sewell, Grumman's chief test pilot and the first pilot to fly the X-29. Sewell was tragically killed in a plane crash on August 4, 1986, when the restored World War II aircraft he was piloting experienced engine failure shortly after takeoff.

Toward Tomorrow

Previous page: Grumman has been selected by NASA to evaluate and manage the companies selected to design and build a manned space station. As the space station program support contractor, Grumman will also develop test requirements for verification assembly and overall integration of space station components. NASA's Dual-Keel Space Station is seen here in its inital operation configuration. It includes two U.S. modules, the European Space Agency module and the Japanese experiment module. It would take 17 Shuttle missions to assemble the station in this configuration. As a member of one of the work package teams, Grumman will design the Space Station crew's living quarters and personal hygene facilities.

Grumman in the latter part of the 1980s remains a technology-driven company. Its products include military aircraft, space exploration vehicles, data processing and information systems, and surveillance systems. All are technology-dependent.

In 1984 Grumman was restructured to meet the requirements of new markets, and to deploy its many advanced capabilities to the best effect. Its 33,000 people are grouped into ten operating divisions: Aircraft Systems, Aerostructures, St. Augustine, Melbourne Systems, Electronics Systems, Space Systems, Technical Services, Data Systems and Allied. A Space Station Program Support division was established in 1987. The new structure assures customers that their concerns are of paramount importance to the Grumman divisions with which they do business. It makes the company more efficient and more flexible.

Aircraft Systems manufactures military aircraft; it is by far the largest division. There are roughly 130 aircraft on a U.S. Navy aircraft carrier: almost 80 per cent of those airplanes are built by Grumman.

In addition to the upgrades of the F-14, A-6, E-2C and EA-6B, Grumman is also studying technologies that will be critical to the next generation of tactical aircraft. These include aeroelastic structures, non-metallic structures, advanced virtual cockpit, digital flight control, complex signal/data processing, high-speed data buses, low observables, full mission simulation and much more. The company is also making the necessary investment to maintain its preeminent position in airborne early warning. Conformal radar, adaptive detection and phased array are part of this effort, and the company is studying arrangements that could be adapted to both Navy and Air Force requirements.

Aerostructures handles the subcontracting work that Grumman does for other aerospace companies. Grumman St. Augustine, which takes its name from the Florida city where it is located, specializes in the overhaul and modification of aircraft, serving the military and commercial markets.

Melbourne Systems, located in Melbourne, Florida, is headquarters for Joint STARS – Joint Surveillance and Attack Radar System – which Grumman is developing for the U.S. Air Force and the Army. Joint STARS will provide real-time surveillance of the battlefield and rear echelons to detect, identify and track enemy armor and vehicular traffic. It will provide their locations to appropriate Air Force and Army commanders, enabling them to assess intentions and manage attacks. Grumman leads a team that includes United Technologies' Norden Systems and the Boeing Military Airplane Company. The system will be installed in a modified Boeing 707, designated the E-8A. Boeing will renovate the aircraft and Norden will build the radar.

Joint STARS will multiply the effectiveness of tactical weapons. NATO nations are being briefed on this far-reaching program. A number of other countries are also interested, and the market for Joint STARS is estimated at $10 billion over the next 10-15 years.

What is especially interesting about this contract is that Norden, a leading radar house, is developing and building the Joint STARS radar system to Grumman's design. Increasingly, this is the pattern of Grumman's work in electronics. As requirements for sophisticated military systems have become more and more specific, Grumman has

had to develop more expertise in the components that make up that system. It is no longer enough to know where to shop for them: Grumman has found it useful to be able to design the components and have a supplier build them.

Melbourne Systems and the Electronics Systems divisions are first cousins: they are related to the systems integration experience Grumman gained through the development of its aircraft. The company has integrated sophisticated electronic systems into more aircraft types than any other company in the world. Grumman aircraft have twice the electronics content by weight of their counterparts anywhere.

Above: Grumman has one of the world's best anechoic chambers in which electromagnetic emitters such as radars, jammers, and similar devices can be tested without interference or detection. This chamber plays a major role in the upgrading of EA-6B Prowler and EF-111A Raven electronic countermeasures systems.

Right: Robotic manufacturing is being used to assemble wings at Grumman. Here a specially programmed ASEA arm is riveting a section of wing flap.

Opposite top: Stacking gallium arsenide slices before the start of the chip manufacturing process.

Opposite upper center: This Grumman gallium arsenide microelectronic circuit is the tiny dot surrounded by silver electrical connections.

Opposite lower center: A single space-based radar element, each of which is individually steerable, not mechanically but electronically.

Opposite bottom: A small part of the gigantic "roller blind" which forms the future space-based radar.

Below: An engineer at Grumman Data Systems works with a light pen to perfect a design for a robotic manufacturing work station.

automatic test equipment, space programs, surveillance, missiles, displays and trainer products. Defense electronics is the fastest-growing segment in Pentagon budgets. Over one third of the Department of Defense budget for procurement, research, development, test and evaluation is for electronic equipment and systems.

For the U.S Army, Grumman is developing the next generation of automatic test equipment. The Army will be able to use this equipment right on the battlefield to detect faulty components in the electronics of weapons systems. It will be adaptable to anything in the Army's arsenal, eliminating the need for the hundreds of different testers now in use.

Central to the development of any electronic system are microchips, tiny devices of almost unbelievable complexity. Most of today's commercial chips are etched into wafers of silicon, but a rapidly emerging new technology replaces the silicon with gallium arsenide. Grumman has established its own gallium arsenide design and fabrication center, called Tachonics, at a site in New Jersey adjacent to Princeton University. Gallium arsenide chips are more resistant to heat and radiation than their silicon counterparts, and they function better at higher frequencies – which makes them well suited to military applications. In addition to supplying Grumman, Tachonics will produce custom chips for commercial sale.

The Space Systems division is working on space surveillance for the Department of Defense, and manned space programs for NASA. The most significant of the military projects is the Boost Surveillance and Tracking System for the U.S. Air Force. The system will be able to detect and track missiles during their boost phase, which is immediately after launch. A Grumman-led team will compete with a Lockheed Corporation team for a contract to build an experimental flight-test satellite.

The Grumman design for a Boost Surveillance and Tracking System is based on a technology the company started working on in the 1970s: a mosaic starer sensor system.

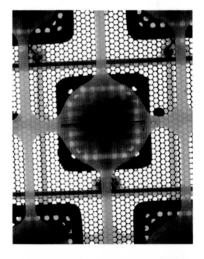

Increasingly, the electronics inside a satellite are just as important as the platform that carries them. Not so many years ago, the company that built the satellite would be the prime contractor, and those that built and integrated the electronics would be the subcontractors. But with the Boost Surveillance and Tracking System, Grumman – the prime — would develop the sensors and integrate them with the spacecraft; Rockwell, one of Grumman's subcontractors, will build the vehicle.

Another project is space-based radar, which Grumman has been working on for over a decade. One version calls for an antenna consisting of thousands of electronically steered elements. The antenna would be flexible and lightweight. It could be rolled up, much like a window shade, and stowed in the launch vehicle; then it could be unfurled in space and put to work. Power would come from electricity generated by vast arrays of solar collectors and solar cells carried on a mast.

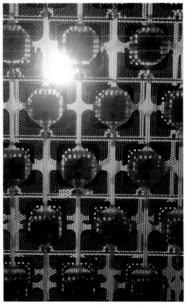

In civil space, the Space Station Program Support division was awarded an $800 million contract to assist NASA in the overall integration of the manned space station project—including evaluation

and management of four companies that have been selected to design and build the space station. As the program support contractor, Grumman will also develop test requirements for verification, assembly and overall integration of space station components.

Grumman is also a member of one of the NASA manned space station work package teams concentrating on outfitting the space station crew's living quarters.

The Technical Services division is a subcontractor to Lockheed as a member of the Shuttle Processing team, which readies the shuttle for successive flights. Grumman manages a network of launch processing system computers along with instrumentation, software, ground support, and measurement and calibration labs.

The Data Systems division designs, installs, operates and supports computer systems for management information. Under contract to Rolls-Royce, Ltd., of Bristol, England, Grumman is designing a computerized jet engine test support system. It will link 30 test groups in two cities, reducing the time it takes to develop and test a new engine. Grumman has worked on more than 20 systems of this type; customers include NASA's Marshall Space Flight Center and the U.S. Air Force's Arnold Engineering Development Center.

The division is also making inroads in the computer maintenance and repair business, and now has offices from coast to coast.

One of the company's largest contracts belongs to the Allied Division: a $1.1 billion agreement to build 99,150 aluminum trucks for the U.S. Postal Service. An option for an additional 59,490 trucks could bring the total to $1.8 billion. Grumman is the world's largest producer of aluminum truck bodies; it has been in this business since 1946.

As diverse as these businesses seem, they are all outgrowths of opportunities and technologies Grumman has been developing for years.

The next century will see great advances made in the development and performance of aircraft and spacecraft, and in communication and surveillance systems. A key reason for these advances will be the increasing capacity and speed of computers, coupled with the decreasing size of computer components.

Space-based and airborne receivers will gather strategic information such as the location of troops, aircraft, missiles and ships. Data concerning global weather patterns will also be collected. This information will be instantly available to a worldwide communications network.

Artificial intelligence systems aboard ships and aircraft and on land will sort this information and assist military leaders in identifying targets and in establishing critical offensive and defensive priorities.

Artifical intelligence systems will be particularly valuable to aircraft pilots who must make quick decisions based on vast amounts of incoming data. Pilots will also be assisted by voice-activated weapons and emergency systems. High-resolution in flight vision systems will greatly improve all-weather navigation, targeting and attack capabilities.

Electronic systems aboard high performance aircraft will "heal" themselves by transferring work from faulty or battle-damaged components to other equipment.

Fiber optics will make aircraft electronic systems lighter, more reliable and less vulnerable to jamming and other interference. Fiber optics will also eliminate the heat that now builds up within closely packed electronic components.

Stealth technology will make future aircraft virtually invisible to radar, and jet engines that run cooler and more efficiently will be less susceptible to infrared detection and identification. Advances in jet engine technology will give aircraft the ability to cruise routinely at speeds exceeding Mach 1. And the widespread use of advanced composites will make aircraft lighter, stronger and more fuel efficient.

Man will return to the moon to establish a permanent base for scientific studies. Living in space will become accepted practice as nations undertake programs to understand the evolution of the universe and our solar system. Robotic systems aboard satellites will assist greatly in the exploration of space - especially the study of planets.

Efforts to break through the time and speed barriers will increase, and travel to the nearest stars could become a reality.

Grumman is poised to take an active part in the design, development and manufacture of the most advanced aerospace and electronic systems of the 21st century. The company and its people will maintain the drive to innovate, the experience to succeed and the determination make a critical difference in the world tomorrow.

Below: Grumman's space-based radar could play a central role in future SDI efforts. The radar's antenna would be unrolled in space like a gigantic window blind. The twin rectangles at one end generate electric power.

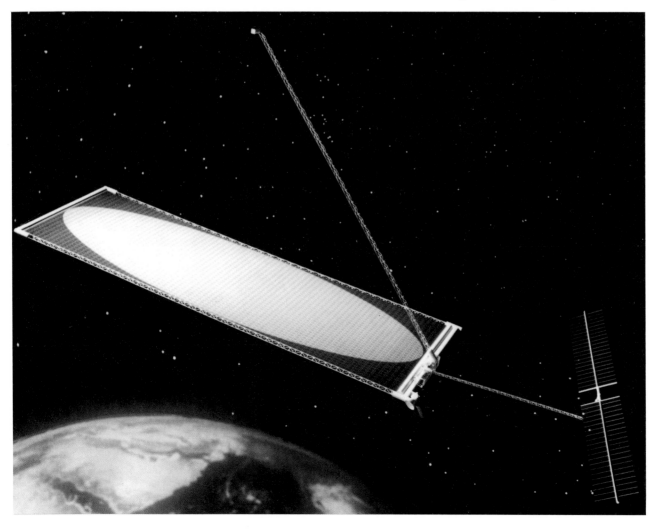

General Index

Grumman Aircraft